SEAN STRNAD

BENNETT

Published by Lulu Press, Inc.
3101 Hillsborough St.
Raleigh, NC 27607-5436

ISBN 978-1-312-24178-7

Printed in the United States of America
First Printing, 2014

Cover design and inside illustrations by the author

Contents

Part I.

Part II.

Part I

I.

"Mr. Shepherd? Did you hear me?"

Bennett fled the lobby, leaving the payphone dangling by its chord, rushing anxiously to his son who was only minutes away from birth. The sweat glands on his palms and forehead opened their flood gates as he ran through the hospital, knocking into a few snappish nurses, nearly toppling a cart full of medication. He stampeded past a doctor sending his clipboard through the air, fighting his way through the controlled chaos to the maternity ward. Outgoing ammonia, urea, salts, and sugars danced in the odorous perspiration of his armpits as if to welcome imminent evaporation. His wife was in labor with their first child and he was going to miss it over a business call—a call, which as it happens, would never yield certain lucrative government contracts for his minting business, which *would* lead to the accruement of huge financial losses. He burst through the door of C-586 and ran to the side of his beautiful Lucia, lying on the bed with a sensuous smile, holding a wet, slimy sea bass.

Immediately, he awoke, coming to his senses in a dark chilly room. He'd been in a deep slumber, captivated by one of his recurring dreams. Moisture ran down his head as he sighed, scanning the ceiling, his pupils adjusting to the pitch-black space that enclosed him. Obscure jabber trickled in from outside the door, a couple of machines beeped and hummed. On top of that, his ears discerned another body resting a few feet from his bed, wheezing faintly beneath each breath.

Why the hell was she holding a sea bass? Bennett wondered. For a second he felt he might be in the same hospital room where his ex-wife had given birth, in the same bed. This was not the case, of course, though it was more comparable than he would have preferred. Most hospital rooms look familiar and a hospital room was exactly where he lay. He wiped the sweat off his forehead and looked at the clock next to his bed. 4:23 A.M.

He thought about the dream some more, relating it to what really happened in times past. He'd only intended to phone an old friend to share the joyous news of his son's birth. The friend, who worked for the Texas International Guard, had been trying to notify him for days of a possible business deal involving the manufacture of military medals and large sums of cash. Fortunes would have been forever altered. Regrettably, it didn't come to pass. Bennett's pager buzzed and he was forced to drop the phone a moment prior to hearing about it, *still* managing to miss his son's birth. Another company ended up getting the contract and did quite well after that. His did not. He often speculated to what length politics were involved in the decision but none of that mattered *now*. He closed his eyes and drifted back to sleep.

"Born on March 6, 1956, at 4:23 A.M.," a female voice said amidst a circle of blue scrubs. Though nothing more than a mental abstraction —that is, lacking a genuine sonic quality — he perceived the words with an intensity that made them feel utterly real.

"Six pounds, two ounces."

That's my birthday, he thought, instantly noticing his father standing next to the bed.

"Doc?" one of the nurses said to him. "Do you want me to get this tray out of here now?"

Looking at the nurse bewildered, he realized was wearing a blue scrub, blue pants, a blue cap, and a procedural mask—he was the maternity doctor.

"I'll take it," he said, staring at his father, always there for his mother as he'd meant to be for Lucia. I wonder where my siblings are? he pondered. Bennett had an older brother and sister. He would eventually get a baby brother but that was not until he was in first grade, which at this particular instant felt like neither past nor future. He departed from the hospital room and found that the door led not to a corridor inside the maternity ward but instead quiet Main Street in downtown Tomball, Texas, the city where he grew up. He stood on the sidewalk, still looking the part of a doctor in his blue garb though no longer holding the tray. Unfamiliar faces passed him without paying any notice. He felt like a ghost.

He turned around to the door he'd exited from, recognizing the big sign that towered over it: "Teddy's Hamburgers." He knew the place well, Teddy's being his favorite diner as a young boy until its doors closed in 1967. He and his older brother and father regularly ate there back in those days. His father would order the same thing every time: a double stacked Angus beef with caramelized onion and steak sauce. It became Bennett's favorite too.

He went over to a large window and took a peek inside. There he was, with his father and brother, a much younger version of himself, maybe eight or nine if he had to guess. The three stopped eating their hamburgers and fries and at once shifted their attention to him glaring through the window, incredulous and confused. They pointed their fingers and broke out into hysterics, laughing to the point of tears. Agitation pierced him, a feeling of fear but not quite as primal. It was more like uneasiness. Police sirens began blaring in the distance, growing louder, approaching like a buoyant parade until they drowned out all other sensations.

Then he woke up to the sound of a newscast.

"He's turning down Sunset Boulevard! Oh! Oh my! This footage is simply incredible!"

Bennett squinted his eyes until his vision became clear. He re-

[11]

calibrated his sense of position in the Universe. He was awake now, back in *his* hospital room, light shining through the window, in front of him on a television screen a live high-speed police chase. Television gold. He could tell the reporter covering it knew so as well. It was the enthusiasm in her announcements:

"Oh my god! He almost hit a car! Pedestrians are running out of the way!"

How pathetically excited she sounded, her lack of concern for anything but her ratings obvious to him.

"Good mornin'" said a raspy voice to his left.

He looked over. A small man, appearing to be in his mid-seventies, shriveled and tanned with freckles on his bald head, sat in another bed.

"They brought you in last night. You my new roommate?"

Bennett smirked. "No, I don't think so. I think I'll be going home today."

"Oh," the man said, disappointed. "They keep bringin' ya people in here and then takin' ya out... I think they doin' it on purpose, like they don't think I'm ever gettin' outta here. They only fuckin' with me but I'll prove 'em wrong, just watch!" His tone quickly turned cross, his attention turning to the mounted TV. "I hope that son of a bitch takes some of them pigs out before they get him! People need to wake up!"

Bennett began to feel uncomfortable.

"Hi Mr. Shepherd," a nurse said, walking into the room.

"Hey hon', can you bring me another orange juice?" the man asked. "I already asked the other guy but he never came back. What's wrong

[12]

with you people?"

"My apologies, Frank. I'll see to it that you get your juice." She looked at Bennett and then began disconnecting him from the heart monitor. "Mr. Shepherd, you can get dressed. Doctor Fischer would like to see you."

He got dressed and followed the nurse.

"Did Frank bother you at all, Mr. Shepherd? He can be a bit, uh," she searched for the right words, "*opinionated* at times."

He smiled and shook his head. As he walked through the hospital, he felt his knees weaken, the walls contract. What's the doctor gotta say? He figured it couldn't be good, vaguely remembering the events of yesterday, becoming ill at work, short of breath, dizzy. He remembered collapsing and waking up at the hospital, being asked about insurance, which his work did not provide, and nurses running tests.

"Have a seat," the nurse said, leading him into the doctor's office. "Doctor Fischer will be with you in a moment."

Bennett waited, his heart fluctuating, unsettled as if claustrophobic butterflies fluttered about inside him. He noted that he was beginning to sweat and upon realizing such, grew more anxious. He peered around the room, distracting himself so as not to induce any further queasiness. A shelf of medical textbooks on one wall and a number of framed awards on the other, the desk in front of him cluttered with papers; this doctor must be pretty damn important, he mused. Bennett wasn't called on by important people. Important people never had any use for him. On some level, briefly dwelling on this made him feel a bit better.

"Morning, Mr. Shepherd," Doctor Fischer said, entering the office. He appeared relatively youthful, vibrant, perhaps in his late forties, early fifties, graying only on the sides of his otherwise impeccable head of hair. He had a dignified look as if his demeanor was borne from the litany of credentials on display.

"I'm assuming you have some bad news, doc? Just give it to me straight."

"Well," the doctor began, "you *did* have a mild heart attack yesterday. Fortunately, it *didn't* cause any further damage to your vital organs. When exactly was the last time you saw a physician?"

"Gee, uh..." Bennett culled his memory. "It had to have been probably ten, fifteen years ago maybe. 2006, I think. Yeah, that's right."

"In that time have you had any leg swelling or trouble breathing? Coughing spouts or..."

"Yeah, sure, I've had some of that. A lot of coughing lately. But I don't have insurance, haven't been in a good position, ya know, financially. And my job doesn't offer it. So I deal with it, ya know? I take some medicine and within a few days, I feel alright. I have an inhaler too."

"Do you smoke?"

"Yeah, occasionally."

"How often is that?"

"I might go through a pack every two, three days. Then I'll go two,

[14]

three days without any. Except at work, people bum 'em out to me every now and then too. Been off and on for a while now though. Can't seem to quit. What did the tests show?"

Doctor Fischer paused, looking down at his papers, then at Bennett, folding his hands on his desk and leaning forward. Bennett had a lump in his throat.

"Mr. Shepherd, the tests showed that you're in very poor health. You have a pleural effusion, too much fluid in the lungs. This would explain the cough, likely brought on by the smoking. But primarily it's your heart, Mr. Shepherd, your heart is enlarged. We've found you have congestive heart failure and it has progressed to stage four."

"How— *how many stages* —how many stages are there? I mean..." Bennett stuttered, his head spinning like a centrifuge.

"It's the end stage. There are no more. You need a heart transplant..."

"A heart transplant? Jesus, how long are we talkin', doc?"

"Well, it's hard to say for sure, different medications and keeping yourself healthy can go a long way. But where you're at presently, if you keep treating your body the way you have been, stressed, *smoking*, not exercising *regularly*, well, we're talking months."

Bennett felt dizzy again. His face turned pale and the chemical compounds beneath his skin once again danced out of his pores.

"Since you don't have insurance," the doctor continued, "our options are going to be limited. However, I know some fine cardiologists and there are a number of excellent organizations that might be able to assist with the costs. I can have someone come in here and talk to you about..."

His voice trailed off while Bennett's mind traveled through deep space, frozen in time. This is what the church works so hard at, preparing their flock for this, he reflected. This is what everything amounts to, ultimately boiling down to moments such as this one. Every human intuitively knows he or she will eventually confront their own demise. All his life he considered the prospect of death and here it finally was, that cold bitch preying on her hapless victim. Now it was real. The doctor nudged his arm.

"Mr. Shepherd? Did you hear me?"

II.

Sara

It was a perfect autumn day in Southeastern Michigan. Only weeks away from Halloween, trees decorated the landscape, abandoning conformity in lieu of various exquisite colors. The city air could not suppress the crisp optimism in nature's changes. Sara sat at the bus stop on Woodward near Maple and waited for transport back to Ferndale, breathing it all in while she read. Books were her escape from the monotony, as was the grandeur of nature, which she relished despite her general dislike of people—a rather frustrating paradox to maintain. She despised what she perceived to be their affection for trivial matters. People, she thought, had devolved to neglect nature's inherent gift of being: being present. People concerned themselves only with past and future, forgetting that *now* is all that ever has been or will be. Nature thrives on living while people thrive on dying; the past deaths of friendships, enemies, memories and the future deaths of jobs, finances, health, and consciousness itself. That's why people make schedules, to note cause and effect, to count their days. Nature composes no notes of yesterday's departure or tomorrow's arrival. It simply is. That was Sara's philosophy.

The book she read was John Steinbeck's classic American novel, *Travels With Charlie*. She envied the author's freedom to unchain himself from the repetition of schedules and travel the heart of America, soaking in the countryside, those winding stretches of two lane roads through forests and mountains, tall luscious oaks on either side, blue lakes, a diversity of fauna in their natural habitat. (To her great disappointment, she later learned that Steinbeck had allegedly made most of the story up from inside his camper which never left his mansion's backyard in Long Island, New York; nonetheless, she admired his depictions.) She pondered that this would be an ideal time to travel. As she sat there patiently waiting for the bus to arrive, two other passengers came and stood nearby. And then another person. And three more. The tranquility of the moment was ruined.

"Who do you have this Sunday for fantasy football?" one man sounded off into his phone. "Oh, *he's* really been sucking!"

"You never do anything *I* want!" a woman to her right bitched, trying to whisper to her man and failing miserably at her attempt to be discreet.

"There you go again, *fucking* ridiculous," he said under his breath.

Another man, very old, sat on the bench next to Sara uttering nonsense. "You gotta go get Harry's vitamins. Larry is coming at two. Gotta be home at one forty-five. It's twelve twenty-eight right now. That gives you an hour. Should call Denise when you get home..." On and on he went.

Finally, the bus arrived and Sara boarded, taking her eyes off her book only when mobility demanded it, intent on retreating into her apartment as soon as possible. She silently rejoiced that the bus load was light and took a seat in an open row near the front. Nobody sat next to her and plenty of empty seats all but guaranteed nobody would, a small victory. The bus coasted along, stopping every few blocks for pickups and drop-offs. On days when Sara rode during rush hour, the ride was terribly unpleasant. Besides her dislike for the bus smell (which brought to mind the foul stench of urine), every time the seats were crammed full, the odor from someone's armpit would linger inches from her face, the stench *especially* foul since most who use public transit also spend much of their day on foot. That's why she preferred window seats. Today wasn't so bad though (today was only urine smell).

Meditating on the words of the novel, she suddenly felt struck by a peculiar instinct. Even as she paid no mind to external distractions, a heavy despair came upon her, a suffocating energy. She glanced up from her book and saw a rugged, lonely man paying for his fare, probably the saddest man she had ever seen. Disenfranchised, desperate, apathetic, a little chubby fellow with droopy eyes and thin gray hair, she recognized him from somewhere but couldn't figure out where. He glanced in her direction and a voice in her head sounded off, repeating: *Please don't sit by me. Please don't sit by me.* Next to her is where the man sat, giving a halfhearted grin as he plopped down before staring off into oblivion. Now that he was right here, she felt obliged to speak up.

"Excuse me," she began hesitantly, "do I know you from somewhere?"

[19]

The dazed man turned his face to hers and spoke softly. "Hmm? No, I don't think so..."

"Wait, *yes I do*. Willow Lane Apartments?"

"Uh, yeah. You live there?"

"Oh my god. Yeah, I think we're neighbors. You live above me."

A light bulb appeared to go off above the man's head and he smiled.

"You're right. I think *I do* recognize you. Bennett," he said, extending his hand.

"Sara."

They shook hands and she sensed he was a person whose company she could genuinely enjoy.

"What'cha reading?" he asked.

"John Steinbeck. *Travels With Charlie.*"

"*The Pearl* is a good one."

"You've read a lot of Steinbeck?"

"No, not really. I like to read, I mean, *some* fiction, but I *prefer* learning things, ya know? Science and that sort."

"Yeah, I enjoy those too. I recently read a book by, um, Michio Kaku, you hear of him? Physicist?"

"Mm-hmm. String theory."

"Yeah," she chuckled, "don't ask me to explain any of that."

Bennett smirked. Sara was quite young, he surveyed, perhaps only twenty-five. She was also very pretty, had a slender face, thick brown hair which she wore in a ponytail, glasses with slim black rims, no jewelry, no makeup, appeared intuitive, free-spirited, exuding an equanimity he couldn't help but appreciate. She reminded him of his daughter in Texas, now in her early thirties, though he hadn't seen her since she was probably Sara's age.

"You know, the bus kind of smells like urine," he said.

She laughed. "Yeah, it does. You ride often? I haven't seen you on before."

"Nah, I got a car. It, uh, broke down at work." This was a lie. But only a white lie.

"Oh, that's a bummer. What do you do?"

"Shop work, at a steel mill. Make parts for different things. Very tedious."

"I bet."

"You?"

"Salvation Army. Going to school too."

"What for?"

"Art therapy."

As they chatted, he forgot about his rotten morning and Doctor Fischer's grim diagnosis. The bus came to their stop a block away from Willow Lane and they got off, walking together, finding one another stimulating, the conversation artless. He walked Sara to her door before he took the stairs to his, shaking her hand again and saying goodbye.

"You know what?" she said.

"Hmm?"

"When you got on the bus, your demeanor, it was distant, heavy,

[21]

like I could feel your energy. It was very... Sad."

"Oh," he said, reminded of his predicament. "It's been, uh, well, it's been an odd day. I wasn't feeling too good. I feel a lot better now though." He smiled and walked up the stairs.

Entering his modest apartment, he took off his work clothes, a black t-shirt and grease-stained khakis. Greeted by a framed print of Linda Mutti's "Sundown on the Meadow" hanging crookedly at the end of the hallway and the wonted fragrance of cigarettes and clutter, he stretched his arms, relieved. Back in his cornsilk colored hive. His cat nudged him, meowing, hungry because he hadn't been home since he left for work the day prior. He apologized as she gazed at him, mewing ever more desperately.

"Okay, okay. Here you go, Mya."

He left a bowl of canned chicken bits on the floor, went into his room, and fell backwards onto the bed. He stared at the ceiling and lit a cigarette, thinking about his heart. He put the cigarette out. He thought about the discussion with the doctor, needing surgery, weekly check-ups, medication, having only a small amount of money he'd saved in the bank—about ten grand, which took him nearly ten years to accumulate.

"Fuck," he said, lighting the cigarette again. "I'm fucked."

Bennett laid there for hours, replaying moments in his life, rehearsing conversations with his estranged family whom he would have to call to inform of his situation. He talked to his therapist about it as she curled up in the blanket next to his arm.

[22]

"Shit's fucked up, Mya. I'm dying. Doctor said the waiting list for a transplant could be months. Said I should ask to get financial help from some fuckin' charities. I dunno what to do, Mya. I think I just gotta accept the fact that it's my time. I'm sorry, baby. I don't wanna leave."

He stroked Mya's head, pressed his face into her fur, and began to sob. She slept gracefully, unmoved by the flow of tears she absorbed; maybe there was a bit of tiger in her. After some time passed, his pity party was interrupted by the ring of his cell phone. He didn't want to answer it but he had no choice. It was his foreman.

"Hey John," he said, wiping his eyes.

"Ben, how ya doin' buddy? I've been tryin' to reach you, called the hospital to see if you were still up there. I was gonna come and see ya."

"They let me come home today."

"What did they say happened? Everyone here thinks you had a heart attack. We weren't sure if you were gonna make it man."

"Yeah, it was a mild heart attack. Doctor said I'm pretty fortunate."

"Shit, they give ya meds or anything?"

"Yeah, I got a prescription for a blood thinner and somethin' else for my heart."

"How ya feel?"

"Not great."

Bennett couldn't keep it in any longer. He decided to tell John about his prognosis. After all, at this point, what did it matter? But he never got the chance.

"Hey Ben, sorry, I gotta let ya go, Fred's callin', he got a part jammed

[23]

up. Take the rest of the week off and see how ya feel Monday."

"Alright, John. See ya then."

Bennett hung up, grateful for John's support. He decided it better that he didn't know. If he could continue to simply pretend he wasn't dying, perhaps it wouldn't be so bad. He got up, threw on a shirt and shorts, and walked into the kitchen, Mya following. He sat down at his café table and chain-smoked while he looked out the window at the city, the sun sinking into the horizon. He knew the next few weeks and months were going to be a battle. No, it would be a war. He knew he was going to die. He knew this fact his entire life. Everyone does. Now he was in death's crosshairs. His time had been determined.

And *he* was determined to die with dignity.

III.

Alfredo, wings, and Ping Pawn

Throughout Bennett's six-plus decades he'd often heard the cliché, "You don't have to find out you're dying to start living." He'd heard of people whose life experiences were enriched upon learning they were terminally ill, as if liberated, having nothing left to lose, granted a *sense* of freedom previously unknown. The further he chewed it over, he came to see that terminal illness could be a sort of born-again experience, albeit obtained later than he would have preferred. He sang a little tune while he slaved over the stove, stirring a packet of Parmesan Alfredo, chicken wings roasting in the oven, the aroma permeating his one bedroom apartment.

"If you want to sing out, sing out. And if you want to be free, be free... cause there's a million things to be, you know that there are..."

Mya must have enjoyed his singing because she slept blissfully on a nearby stool. He sang, growing quieter until a wave of chthonic feelings overcame him. He didn't feel born-again, the existential truth of his condition no less distressing. It was quite the opposite, all of his plans stunted, unable to form even as mere aspirations, wasted opportunities he would never recover, years spent telling himself there was still time. The hairs on the back of his neck stood up as he stared down at the burner, his body paralyzed at the unmasking of reality,

[25]

tears rolling down his cheeks, not wanting to believe he was really leaving earth already though he knew he was.

He pulled himself out of his despair by flipping on the television, the noise a distraction from his meandering thoughts. He found Ping-Pawn, a show about a large family of Asians who own a pawn shop in Chinatown, Manhattan. Eight kids, each one slightly insane like the parents, fighting with each other, breaking merchandise all the while the father and mother hit snags trying to manage the storefront amidst the mayhem. These kinds of shows always made Bennett feel better about himself. He sat down with his Parmesan Alfredo and chicken wings, ranch on the side, and a glass of milk. He finished off the half gallon and would have to go to the grocery store in the morning to get more. He was a lifelong fan of milk.

The phone rang again.

"Hello?"

"Benny, it's Dave."

"Oh, hey Dave."

Dave was a co-worker, a really nice guy but also a big perv. Pretty big drunk too. Still, a really nice guy.

"John told me—er, that you're not coming back 'til Monday and I —I noticed your car was still here..."

"Yeah, I took the bus. Figured I'd ride it in Monday and drive home."

"He also said you had a..."

"Yeah, I'm fine though, really."

"God, talk about a close call! Well, I'm picking up Fred tomorrow. Want me to get the key from ya so we can bring your car over after work?"

"You don't have to do that."

"Nah, it's totally cool. I'm just glad you're alright. I'm about to leave the shop now. It's on the way, I can swing by and get it. Ferndale, right?"

"Really, Dave? Yeah, Willow Lane. Building four, apartment twenty-two, second floor. I appreciate that a lot. Seriously, thanks."

Dave couldn't help but inquire further about the hospital visit so Bennett repeated everything he'd told their boss, sparing details, reluctant to spill the whole truth. Out of all the people he knew he must eventually tell, his co-workers were *not* high priority. When the conversation concluded, he put the phone on the arm of his recliner where he sat and reflected on how pleasant everyone had been today, even though Dave *always was* a *really* nice guy. The nurse, John, Dave, each one of them had been so friendly. John never acted *that* nice. He thought about his neighbor, Sara, a delightful young woman, and his children, Eugene and Sophia. They were both grown now, in their thirties. Eugene worked for the Navy, stationed in South Korea for the past few years, Sophia was a math teacher in Texas. His son would write him every now and then, send Christmas cards, attempt to visit at least once a year. His relationship with his daughter was more tattered and he'd only seen her a handful of times since he'd left Texas. He and his wife Lucia divorced when the children were young. She won custody and when he moved to Michigan it made communication sparse. That was one of his few regrets. He picked up the phone to call his children but set it down.

"I'll wait 'til morning," he commented to Mya, sitting on the couch across from him. Sophia rarely returned his calls and chances were that neither would answer anyway.

Bennett watched mindless television for a while until mocking it grew tiresome. The commercials were too much for him, the people too phony, most of the products too stupid. He pulled a book off his shelf. *The Selfish Gene* by Richard Dawkins.

"I haven't read this in a while."

He leaned back in his recliner, Mya snuggling in his lap. Then came a long, obnoxious, string of taps on the front door.

"Hey Dave," he said, opening it up.

"Benny!"

Bennett noted the stench of alcohol on his breath.

"Sorry, I would've been here earlier but some of the guys invited me out to Laplace's for a couple of drinks."

"It's alright, Dave. Here's the key." Bennett handed Dave his car key, keen on getting the point across: he didn't want extended company.

"Smells good in here," Dave remarked. "Chicken?"

"Yeah, I had some a little while ago. Just gettin' ready for bed actually, doctor said..."

"Yeah, yeah, no problem. I'll bring it by tomorrow, probably seven,

seven thirty-ish."

"Fantastic. Again, thanks a lot for doing this. I really do appreciate it."

"Of course! Get some rest, I'll see ya tomorrow."

Dave walked out and Bennett locked up, resting his back on the door momentarily to acknowledge Dave's parting. He also needed to catch his breath. Making his way back to his recliner, he suffered a coughing spasm. Jesus, he thought, each cough is a reminder I'm a dead man. Whereas before he could blame such things on smoker's cough or old age, now it felt like each one was a death sentence, alerting him that organs were rapidly failing, the worst of it in his imagination. He'd always been somewhat of a hypochondriac—at least that's all he could console himself with. He searched for his inhaler, located it wedged in the chair cushion, then reclined again, Mya rejoining his lap, one arm behind his head. A short time passed and before he could realize it, *The Selfish Gene* fell onto his chest, his muscles fully relaxed, his eye lids sealed shut. And from his nostrils came a thunderous snore.

He stood in the living room of his childhood home in Tomball, Texas, his father on the couch, feet propped on the coffee table.

"You know dad," his sister said as she walked past the living room, "Mom's gonna have a fit if she comes home and sees your feet up there like that."

[29]

"She's not coming home," his father snapped.

"Bennett," his mother's quiet voice chimed in.

He turned around. In the corner sat his elderly mother, her lips quivering, bobbing back and forth in her rocking chair with a rosary clutched to her chest. This dream had often haunted him from deep within his subconscious and he anticipated the words that would come next.

"How's your brother doing, Bennett? Have you talked to Jack lately?"

Jack was Bennett's older brother. He died in 1979 from a speedball overdose, a fatal mixture of heroin and cocaine, forever remaining twenty-seven years old.

"Mom, Jack is not doing anything. He's dead, remember?"

His mother started wailing.

"Bennett, what the *hell* is wrong with you?!" his father shouted. "Don't upset your mother like that! Can't you see she's sick?!"

"Bennett!" his younger brother Sam called from the kitchen. "Come sit down."

Bennett reviewed the house, recalling almost every arrangement and every detail; where each picture frame hung, the color of the curtains, the dusty fireplace they never used, the expensive chinaware his mother kept in a glass display that had gone untouched his entire life. These impressions never left him. It's where he grew up, childhood, high school, as a young adult. He lived here until he married Lucia. He entered the kitchen and stood at the end of a table,

Lucia across from him, bawling her eyes out, Sam on the left and his sister Marcy on the right. Sam spoke gently but sternly, betrayed by the nervousness in his voice from having to confront his elder brother.

"Take a seat, we need to talk with you."

As soon as Bennett sat down, Marcy let him have it.

"Bennett, what the fuck is wrong with you?! What're you thinking?"

Lucia couldn't bring herself to look at him, howling relentlessly, her face buried in a tissue.

"Look," Bennett began to say, "we've had problems for..."

Marcy cut him off. "This whore is what, twenty?!"

"Twenty-two. For Chrissakes, look!" He stood up. "I don't have to listen to this shit! What, Marcy, mom and dad pass and all of a sudden *you're* in charge of the family?"

"Well, apparently the only thing you do is drink! It's like you're turning into mom! You're losing everything!"

"You know what? *Fuck you!*" He turned to Sam.

"Look, Ben..."

"No, Sam, fuck you too!" And then looking towards Lucia: "And fuck you for setting this whole thing up! This is a private matter! Yeah, we've had problems!" he sneered at his siblings. "We've had problems for a *long* time! Did you tell them about kissing the keyboard player at church, Lucia?"

She sobbed even harder.

Sam glanced at her and then Bennett. "Bill? Bill Stephens? *That* guy?"

"Fuck all of you, I'm outta here." He did an about-face and stormed out.

"Bennett! Ben, wait!" Sam called, running out the door. "What about your kids, man? *Think* about 'em. You're throwing your life away. You're turning against the Lord. He won't let you get away with it!"

Bennett turned around. "I love my kids, Sam, but things are complicated. And save the other bullshit, I don't believe a single word of that anymore. I haven't for a while."

"What do you mean?"

He was stunned. Bennett had attended church with his family every Sunday. Everybody they knew thought he was a devout Christian. Sam was. Lucia was. The whole immediate family was (Marcy was the "least religious" and even she prayed under the assumption that a divine being always listened and occasionally responded).

"God isn't real."

Mya rammed her small head into Bennett's face. He woke up, only for a second, startled to realize he'd returned to the present. He'd endured similar flashbacks many nights over the past twenty-six years. They always felt so authentic, like a time warp sending him back to yesteryear. His affair was the straw that broke the family's back, largely responsible for severing their relationship. Half asleep, he thought about it fleetingly and then moved from his recliner to his bed, Mya close behind, flopping down on his blankets. The snoring resumed.

He was driving along in his '86 Grand Am, his eleven-year-old son in the passenger seat and his seven-year-old daughter in the back. His son wouldn't even look at him, well aware of his father's iniquities.

"Where ya going, daddy?"

"Sophia darling, daddy's gotta go away for a little bit," he answered. "He's got a really good job in Detroit and has to take it so he can still buy nice things for you, like that big doll house you want, and go nice places with you, like Sea World. You *do* wanna go to Sea World still, right?'"

"Yeah! Daddy?"

"Yes, Sophia?"

"Eugene said you got a new wife."

Bennett glanced at Eugene. "No sweetie," he said, his eyes meeting Sophia's through the rear-view mirror. "Daddy has a friend."

Eugene uttered something under his breath.

"What's that, Gene?"

"Why don't you tell the truth?! You don't love mom anymore! *You* don't love us!"

[33]

Bennett hit the brakes hard, careening to the side of the road and putting the car in park. He turned to his children. "Now listen to me, I don't want to hear a goddamn word like that ever again!"

"You said a bad word!" Sophia said.

"I'm sorry, daddy *did* say a bad word. But I *mean* it. I'm only going away for a short while. And you guys'll come visit."

"Mom said only if we *want* to," Eugene said.

Sophia looked at him with a venerating smile. "*I* want to daddy!"

Bennett's imagination switched frames, no longer in a car but instead on a sofa at his much younger girlfriend's house, the "college kid." His girlfriend's name was Angel but that was a misnomer. She was biting her bottom lip, fidgeting with her hair. She held a glass of chardonnay, mischief in her eyes, every inch of her embodying sexual vitality. She put her legs on either side of his and sat down on his lap, her breasts level with his face. He kissed Angel on her neck.

"I can't go to Detroit, baby."

She pulled away. "Why not? I *told* you everything. Your divorce will be finalized next month! What're you gonna do? Stay here?"

"I'm talking about my kids. I can't leave *them*. And plus, I've never really seen myself selling mortgages..."

"Sweetie," she said, setting her glass of wine on the table beside her. "You'll be able to have anything you want. And you'll have me. Do it for a year or two. We'll get you the best lawyers, we'll get shared custody, they'll be able to spend summers with us..." She slowly slid down to his belt and began to undo it.

[34]

"I gotta think about... whoa... ah, damn... yeah... fuck... goddammit I love you..."

The sunlight through Bennett's window stirred him awake. In a daze, he got up from his bed and looked at his phone. 9:21 A.M. He sat and recollected his senses, his limbs numb, his chest tight. A flood of sentimentality saturated him; sadness, confusion. He felt as if he didn't understand anything, why he still dreamt about his ex-wife, his ex-girlfriend, all of it so far removed in the past. Though he *had* run into Angel's brother at the fruit market some months earlier, nevertheless he failed to relate with his former self.

"Why do I *still* think about you?" he asked aloud. "It's pathetic..."

He got up, fed Mya, showered, shaved the little facial hair he could grow, and settled at his table, smoking his last cigarette. As he fully awakened, the emotions that carried over from his dream gradually disappeared and he began to feel at ease, even optimistic. He considered the things he ought to do with his morning: buy some groceries, milk, cigarettes, get his prescriptions filled. He didn't have his car but he could walk, both the grocery store and the pharmacy were within a mile. It will be good for you, ya old man, the voice in his head declared. He put on an old sweatshirt, checked his wallet, threw a shoulder bag over his neck, and left the apartment. It was the first day of his new short life.

[35]

IV.

Death is the sound of distant thunder at a picnic

Bennett strolled along Woodward and then down east Nine Mile. The city was alive, cars honking, each hurrying along to his or her job, driven to madness from a tiring week and the tease that a weekend was mere hours away. Birds chirped, intent on migration, squirrels quarreled in the grass, deer hid in backyard bushes and public parks. The street lights flickered off, the sun fully aroused, cracks in the concrete giving way to ants and other insects responsive to the waning bustle of footsteps. Bennett beamed, feeling youth in his bones, waving to strangers, assisting a woman who dropped a briefcase scoop up a few loose papers before they scurried down the block. He dropped off his prescriptions, went to the grocery store, bought milk, eggs, peanut butter, a loaf of bread, ground beef, a bundle of apples, and pickles. Slinging his full bag over his shoulder, he window shopped at a nearby thrift store while waiting for his scripts. There he saw a slightly used new age boombox and a tea pot with a retro floral pattern that reminded him of the bathroom wallpaper in Angel's father's house. When his pill bottles were in hand, he walked home, a pep in his step, humming The Beatles' "Because" along the way.

He looked at his watch as he walked into the parking lot of Willow

Lane and had no idea what to do with the rest of his day. It wasn't even noon and he'd already taken care of everything. The only thing left was make phone calls. He walked up the stairs to his apartment door, reached into his pocket for his key, reached into his other pocket, his back pocket, his grocery bag. He did not have it. His heart sputtered as he grew more anxious, working harder for each pump. He retraced his steps to the pharmacy, eyes glued to the cement. This time he paid no mind to the concrete jungle around him. He asked at the counter, no luck; went to the service desk at the grocery store, nothing; and then the thrift shop. Again, nada. Dejected, he returned home.

"Be back at 2 P.M." the sign on the maintenance door read.

Walking over to the staircase leading to his apartment, he took a seat at the bottom. At least Dave has my car key but what am I going to do now? he deliberated. The despair that plagued him the day before slowly crept over his demeanor, confronted once more with his own mortality. It made no sense to him. Shock and gloom coalesced into anger. But then lady luck seemed to change her tune.

"Bennett?" a familiar voice asked as a door closed behind him.

"Oh, hey Sara."

"What'cha doin'?"

"I locked myself out. Lost my key when I was shopping earlier. And maintenance won't be back until two."

"I'm sorry. If you'd like, you can put your groceries in my fridge. I was just on my way to the art supplies store."

"Oh, that would be great! Really? I don't want to hold you up."

[37]

"No it's fine, plenty of room in there, I'm in no rush. You can come along if you'd like." She paused, unsure what she'd invited him along for, though he seemed harmless enough and their conversation the day prior had been congenial.

He paused too, tired from walking all morning.

"Got nowhere else to be, right?"

They both chuckled

Stepping into her apartment, which reeked of marijuana, she took his groceries and put them in her refrigerator. He looked around, her place full of interesting art, small trinkets, some crafted from wire, others from beads, homemade candles of various colors and sizes. On the walls hung lavish abstract paintings.

"You do these?"

"Yeah. It's kind of an obsession. When I'm not reading, I'm doing something crafty. A lot of painting lately."

"I'm impressed. They're very strange."

Many of her paintings consisted of deformed and frightened faces, surrounded by countless wandering eyes and geometric shapes, colors and swirls with no apparent meaning or purpose, at least as he perceived them. He noticed a signature on one of the pieces.

"S.W.?"

"Sara Wilson. That's my name."

"Ah. Nice place you got, makes mine look boring. You live alone?"

"Mm-hmm. Well, my boyfriend stays over a lot. Hey, do you smoke?"

[38]

"Uh, like, you mean..."

"Yeah, pot," she laughed, turning crimson.

"I haven't in *years*. But sure, why not? I could use a little reefer I suppose."

The two sat down around a bong Sara brought out from her bedroom.

"Wow, that's big," he said.

"Isn't it? This thing gets me blown out!"

They smoked until he could handle no more, coughing relentlessly.

"Careful you don't hack up a lung there," she joked, fetching him a glass of water.

"Shit, I'm stoned..." Indeed, the bong left him feeling euphoric, his heart racing almost as fast as his thoughts.

"Hey!" she said, out of the blue. "I have an idea!"

"What's that?"

"Why don't I bring some of those apples you bought, make us sandwiches, and we can have a picnic at Davis Park!"

He was pleased with the idea if not a bit curious. After all, even though they were neighbors, they'd only formally met twenty-four hours earlier.

"You're serious?"

"Yeah! C'mon, it will be fun! You don't have to go to work or something, do you?"

"Nope, took the day off. Had—had a bad migraine this morning. You?"

[39]

"I don't work on Fridays. Usually I have school but my professor had a funeral to go to."

"Oh. Well, lucky you. Where's your boyfriend? Does he want to come along?"

"He's at work. He's always at work. He doesn't have *time* for picnics."

"Gotta make a living, ya know? You said yesterday that you're going into art therapy?"

"Yes sir."

"I bet that's rewarding."

"Yeah, it's kind of odd though. I generally don't like people but I love art and I enjoy other people's art, so I figured, ya know, maybe it could be therapeutic for me as much as it is for them."

"That's insightful. Why don't you like people?"

"What's there to like? We're a stupid, barbaric species."

He looked at her dubiously.

"People are simple-minded. They go about their routines, only thinking about themselves, convinced of their own greatness. And plus, what other creatures go to elaborate lengths to lie and cheat and kill as we do? Animals do those things out of necessity, to survive. They *have* to do those things. We don't. We do them as an exercise of power."

"That's deep," he said half-sarcastically. "That's just nature. But I think most people have good intentions."

"I dunno. Either way, they annoy me to no end. The pettiness, the

[40]

monotony of human affairs, it's pointless to me. I dunno, does that sound conceited?"

"Nah. Well, maybe a little."

The two left the apartment complex and walked along Woodward to the art supplies store. Bennett enjoyed Sara's company more and more as they conversed.

"My dream is to travel," she told him. "I want to get out of Michigan. I've lived here my whole life."

"That can't be very long."

"Twenty-four years!"

He'd been pretty close, guessing she was twenty-five. "Where ya wanna go?"

"I don't care, anywhere! Like in *Travels With Charlie*, I wanna drive around the country, live out of a camper, no work, no schedules, nothing but freedom and nature, and perhaps a dog to enjoy my adventures with."

He agreed, thinking about a dog he once owned, that did sound delightful. "You'll get to do that one day."

"I doubt it," she said, her attitude hostage to dismay. "I've been working my whole life and barely have anything to show for it. Times are different. People don't get to go on vacations anymore. Only if I win the lottery or marry someone rich... then I'd have enough money to travel anywhere I wanted!"

"You can still get out of Michigan, right?"

"Perhaps, but it's so far down the road at this point."

"You're still young! I didn't leave my hometown until I was thirty-six."

They perused the art store, functioning by instinct as they'd both become lost in each other's words. It was as if time became nonexistent.

"Where are you from?" she asked.

"Texas. Grew up in Tomball, lived in The Woodlands."

"The Woodlands?"

"Yeah, it's about thirty miles north of Houston, has maybe 80-90,000 people. It's not all tumbleweeds and swamps if that's what you're asking," he explained with a laugh.

Sara bought a couple of paint brushes and a few tubes of paint. They walked out of the store and headed towards the park.

"What in heaven's name made you decide to move to Michigan?" she asked.

"Well," he began, "to make a long story short, I had a girlfriend in Texas whose father had his own mortgage firm here in Detroit. She convinced me to move here. I took the job, did pretty well..."

"*You* sold loans?" She looked at him amusingly.

"Yeah. Why do you say it like that?"

"You don't strike me as the sales type. You seem kinda mopey."

"*Mopey?*" He wondered if his depression had been all too obvious.

"No, not mopey, that's not the right word. Like, you're very stoic, doesn't seem like you'd have enough enthusiasm for something like that. Who would want to buy mortgages from Eeyore?!"

He rolled his eyes. "Gee, thanks. Actually, I did quite well but you're right, I hated it. It drove me crazy. The only thing that kept me in it was—"

"The money?"

"Yeah. Before that I minted custom coins."

"So, you're an artist!"

"Kinda, yeah, I guess I am."

When they arrived at the park, Sara rolled out a blanket, setting out their sandwiches and apples and canned lemonade she'd brought. It was a lovely fall afternoon, the sun reflecting off the leaves to create a near perfect image, like something one might see on a post card. A couple of joggers ran the perimeter of the park, a mother watched as children climbed across old monkey bars.

"It's gorgeous out today, isn't it?"

Bennett's mind had wandered. He was caught up in the past, thinking about Angel and his successes as a loan officer, about minting coins and Texas, his heart, his mortality.

"Bennett?"

"Huh? Sorry."

"You looked lost there for a minute."

He sighed and lit up a cigarette. "Yeah... Hey, can I ask you somethin'?"

"Sure, of course."

"Promise you won't think it's a weird question?"

"I promise."

"What do you think of... death?"

"Like, you mean, what do I think happens after you die?"

"Yeah."

"Gosh... um," she hesitated, contemplating. "I dunno. Personally, I try not to think about it. I guess when people die, that's it, ya know? Maybe there's a hereafter, like our spirit or something goes on somewhere, or maybe not. I'm not against the idea but who can say for sure? I don't think I believe in God or anything if that's what you mean. Why ya ask about *that*?"

"Nothin' really..." He had another coughing spasm, far worse than anything Sara had witnessed earlier.

"Are you okay?"

"Yeah, I'm fine..." He concluded it was time to tell her, to tell himself, to put it 'out there' in the world, make it 'real.'

"Okay, look. The truth is I'm sick. Actually, no, I'm dying... Found out yesterday... Heart disease, it's very far along, doctor gave me a few months..."

"Oh my goodness! I'm so sorry. I never would have asked you to —"

"Smoke? Nah, I needed it. I didn't wanna say anything. I didn't want you to pity me or whatever. I haven't wanted to tell anyone. It doesn't seem real yet. I dunno how to make sense of it..." He trailed off.

She struggled to find the words. She wanted to console him but what could she say? Sorry about your luck, stranger? Hey, I'm sure it's nothing?

[44]

"So why are ya smoking?" she asked.

"I don't think it makes much of a difference now. The doctor said I'd need a transplant and it's unlikely I'll get one. No insurance. People a lot younger than me, from families with money, probably need 'em more than I do anyway."

"What about your family? Can't *they* help you?"

Bennett looked down. "No family out here. They're all in Texas, well, except my son, he's in the Navy. I wouldn't burden them with that anyway, leave them in debt, as if I haven't caused enough turmoil already."

Strangers often told Sara about their problems. They found her easy to trust with personal details because she knew how to feign interest, a skill she had perfected to a tee. However, it was different with Bennett, she was truly intrigued by him.

"Caused enough turmoil?"

"Shit, well when I moved here years ago, I left my marriage, my kids. My family has always resented me, *not that I can blame them*. I dunno why I'm tellin' ya this, I shouldn't bore you with my problems."

"No, it's okay," she said. "You can tell me anything you want. What're *your* feelings about, uh—"

"Death?"

"Yeah. You don't have to answer that if you don't want to."

He scratched his head, looking around at the trees, the clouds, the surrounding city. "I think it's the greatest mystery, the great unknown... the thing that plagues everybody's subconscious, an instinctive fear that compels all other thoughts and emotions, ya know? Nobody wants to admit there's no afterlife, no 'there' to get to, but that's probably the case. There's a quote by Emerson, he said, 'Death comes to all, but great achievements build a monument which shall endure until the sun grows cold.' That's my problem. I don't have any great achievements. I've always told myself that death is a natural process, like birth or aging, that there's nothing to fear. But deep down I *do* fear it. I don't want my existence to be defined as an insignificant statistic, a random name in the local obituary noticed only by a small handful of people who cared about me. My motivation was that life was still in front of me, there was still time, I could still do somethin' incredible, to —"

"Find meaning?" she interjected.

"Exactly. As circular as it sounds, the meaning of my life was the search, *my search* for meaning. *That* made sense to me and now I feel like it's gone. I'm only existing, waiting to die." His eyes began to water.

"'The fear of death follows from the fear of life,'" she whispered. She looked at him and smirked. "Mark Twain."

"What's that mean?"

"It means you can't really embrace the inevitable until you've learned to accept—no, appreciate—the evitable, to live life to the fullest. Sure, you can live a life full of years but that won't satisfy you. What is that thing—that one thing—you've always wanted to do? Could *anything* ever satisfy your search? Could you ever 'make it there,' to whatever it is you're looking for?"

[46]

He smiled. "Good question. I've always wanted to write a book."

"What kind of book?"

"I dunno... Somethin' that could really impact people, *change* things..."

"You mean like wake people up?"

"Yeah, ya know, inspire them, get people thinking about their lives differently, to realize this life is all we have, that we ought to utilize every minute of it in the hopes that somethin' better will be left behind for the next generation..."

"Perhaps you needed to think about your life differently first. I take it you don't believe in a hereafter?"

"No, I don't. Heaven, hell, gods, faeries, they're nothing more than useless toys devised by the human brain. Sure, they serve a purpose to *some*, but when I look out at the world and the impact these sorts of ideas have had on it, I feel nothing but vitriol towards mystical thinking, religious dogmas, all that nonsense."

"What's *your* biggest problem with it?"

"Where to begin? Well, I grew up very religious, had it ingrained in me from the earliest moments I can remember. It's funny, I haven't been to church in years and I can still recite the verses, the stories, the songs. And I was taught that the person who questions the existence of God, who rejects faith, is going to burn in hell forever and ever. A lot of children are told this. The effects are devastating. You're burdened with tremendous amounts of unnecessary duress that can only be cured by total submission to the delusion, or so one is taught. It's fear-mongering at its worst. I think it forced me to suppress my curiosity, view the world as evil, deceived, helpless without God. I mean, what good can come from that? Plus, it advances a general credulity."

"I think I know what you mean. You want people to be independent, to think for themselves, explore who they are without fear of reprisal. Parents should guide their kids on *how* to think, not *what* to think... I get that." She paused for a moment. "Hey Mr. Philosopher, I've got an idea. What're ya doin' tomorrow?"

"Tomorrow? Uh, nothing I can think of..."

"You should come over my place and paint. Put your pain, your fears, all your emotions about your current situation into the paintbrush, get it out of your mind, put it on paper."

"I'm not much of a painter. I'm terrible actually!"

"It's okay, I think it could be really good for you."

"You think so?"

As they sat in the park talking about life, philosophy, religion, a connection developed between them, a friendship, an innocuous and subtle love. Upon returning to Willow Lane that afternoon, Sara spotted something:

"Bennett! Look!"

There on the sidewalk was his apartment key. He couldn't believe he'd missed it. He thanked Sara relentlessly even though she couldn't take credit, got his groceries from her apartment, hugged her, and said goodbye. As he walked into his apartment, he thought about Eugene and Sophia, Sam and Marcy. He would have to call them today. But for now at least the dread had eased.

V.

Dragon's Blood

Dragon's Blood rose to the ceiling, escaping through the screen of an opened window. The incense pierced Sara's nose where she lay, mentally exhausted, smoking a joint. From the time she arrived home, she found herself struggling to read or paint or clean or do anything productive. She lounged on her couch, eyes closed as though she were in a Buddhist temple, contemplating the enormity of her neighbor's quandary. She plucked her ukulele but it felt futile. She'd finished *Travels With Charlie* and determined the next book she would read (for the third time) would be *Siddhartha* by Hermann Hesse. When she picked it up, however, she was unable to think of anything besides Bennett's descent into the unknown. Her mind traversed time, frontiers unfamiliar to her conscious reflection. She didn't like dwelling on her childhood or teenage years, her mother a verbally abusive, haranguing alcoholic, her father a stranger she dismissed as a young woman (resentful over his rejection of her as a child).

Her phone buzzed. It was a text message from her boyfriend: "Be over soon. Do u want me to pick up carry-out from Neumann's?"

She texted him back and continued sulking. "Half of her brain" carried on a conversation with the "other half," the committee called Self-Awareness deliberating among itself:

Do you really care about him? He's your neighbor for crying out loud!

True. And I've only known him since yesterday.

This is why you avoid people. They tell you their problems, you get emotionally attached, and then given the opportunity they take advantage of you!

He's harmless.

Harmless?! You heard what he said, he left his wife... his family!

That was a long time ago. People change. Who am I to judge?

Who are you kidding?

Not to mention, he's dying... It must feel terribly lonely.

It's frightening. You don't want to think about that. It's all about living in the present moment, Sara.

But what is this? Lying to myself? Am I just ignoring my fears? Is there even anything *to* fear? Is there more to life than this?

Why? Should there be?

She rolled another joint and returned to her drawing board, splashing some paint onto a canvas, smearing it around until it became black. In the amalgam of colors that trickled down a picture emerged. She covered the top half in streaks of black and gray and brushes of white; the bottom half was a mixture of red, violet, green, and orange. She formed flowers out of the colors, dotting their leaves with navy blue rain drops falling from the melancholy shade above.

"Hey babe!" her boyfriend called as he walked through the door. "How you doin?" He kissed her and placed a bag of food on the kitchen counter.

"I'm alright. Just painting."

"Oh yeah? Guess what happened at work today!"

Her boyfriend told her about his day, about how Gary in accounting clogged the office toilet with a colossal turd that resulted in shit and piss water spilling everywhere when someone tried to flush it down.

"Everyone in the office got a big kick out of it," he laughed.

She told him about Bennett and her plan to attempt art therapy with him. He thought it was an excellent idea. It helped to talk about her feelings, to free her mind of the empathy she had allowed herself to experience. They ate dinner together and afterward he watched a hockey game, she read *Siddhartha*.

Above them on the second floor, Bennett sat in his recliner, macaroni casserole in hand, watching the same hockey game, the Red Wings versus the Canadians. He'd spent the afternoon on the phone, calling numbers Doctor Fischer had given him, listening to prerecorded messages, consulting with dingbats. Everyone either told him to wait for a call back or to try another extension. When he called his family all he got were more prerecorded messages. He couldn't reach his son in Seoul. He left voicemails with his siblings and daughter, telling them it was urgent, figuring they would call him back sometime. As he got comfortable in his recliner, there was a long, obnoxious, string of taps on the door. He'd forgotten that Dave was coming by with his car.

"Hey guys," Bennett said, opening the door.

"Benny!" the synchronized voices exclaimed. It was Dave and Fred. Dave invited himself in and handed Bennett his car key. Bennett couldn't bring himself to object as Dave had been gracious enough to do him this favor.

"Would either of you like some macaroni casserole?" he asked. "I made enough."

Dave and Fred looked at each other. "Sure!"

Both in their late forties, Fred was a short, stocky, wise guy—as was Dave—except Dave was short and sleek. Their behavior was oftentimes more reflective of two adolescents, displaying a vulgarity and ruggedness that was commonplace at the steel mill; undoubtedly, the place had taken its toll on them. Individuals who've spent the greater part of their lives in a factory tend to forfeit a piece of themselves along the way, at least that's what Bennett supposed (although he understood on the outside others probably thought the same about him as he'd spent the last ten years at the mill as well and couldn't be too confident in his own analysis).

"So I hear you're doin' alright, had a mild heart attack or somethin'?" Fred remarked as he shoveled casserole into his mouth.

"Yeah, but I'm alright. How's everything at the shop?"

"Same old. John put me on your job since he said you ain't gonna be back 'til Monday. I like those machines a lot more than mine."

"That's 'cause you're always jammin' yours up," Dave said.

"It ain't my fault!"

"Oh shit!" Dave exclaimed.

"What?" Fred looked around.

"I forgot to record my show tonight. It's on at nine, we gotta go Fred!"

"What show?" Bennett asked.

"That one, The Investigators, with that little redhead girl, the one with the big tits."

"Heather Block?" Fred asked.

"Mm-hmm. And damn does she have some blocks alright. If I could, I'd take that bitch by her hair and..."

"Alright Dave, c'mon," Fred said, sensing Bennett was becoming annoyed. "Ben, thanks for dinner! Hope ya feel better come Monday."

"I'm sure I will. Thanks again for bringin' my car, Dave."

"No problem, bud."

Bennett walked them to the door and returned to his recliner. His heart didn't feel right. It felt tight, like a butter knife was lodged in his chest. He took his pills, smoked a cigarette, paced around the kitchen, hacked up a lung, sat back down. He looked at his phone and noticed he had missed a call. It was from his brother.

"Well Mya, guess I better call Sam."

He waited anxiously while Sam's phone rang. They only spoke every six months or so and he could never quite predict how conversations with his brother would go. Sam constantly reminded him of what a devout Christian he was. Bennett didn't know if Sam realized he did it or not but it often escalated into a silly debate over the existence of God until eventually someone would gain the better sense to hang up.

"Big brother," Sam answered. "How are you?"

"I'm alright. You?"

There was an awkward pause. "Doing great. Hey, I've been meaning to ask you... Did you get that book I sent you?"

"Which one?"

"Uh, which was it... the, uh, *Suffering Savior* one."

"Sam, you asked me that last time we talked. You sent that a while back."

"I did? Oh, well, did you read it?"

"Yes, I told you that. You don't remember?"

"No..."

"Yeah, we had a whole conversation about it. We talked about Joseph of Arimathea, how he was probably a fictional character placed in the story to account for Jesus' missing body, and how—"

"That's right, you did keep insisting on that."

"I said it was one of many more plausible explanations... Did *you* read the book I sent *you*?"

"The angry atheist one?"

"It wasn't angry. Well, I mean to you, perhaps. But the author was simply documenting the terrible things done in the name of faith..."

"No, I didn't finish that one yet. I've still gotta finish the one you sent me before. I think it was 'Why I Hate God So Much Even Though He's Not Real.'"

[55]

"Ha ha, was that the title? Very funny."

"So what's up brother?"

"Um..." He searched his rehearsed words, dispirited about the response they might invoke. "How's Marcy and Sophia?" he asked instead.

"Sophie's doing great, saw her yesterday actually. She took Sam Jr. and Jimmy out for Sam's birthday."

"That's nice," Bennett said. "Tell him happy birthday for me. He's gotta be gettin' old. Seventeen, eighteen now?"

"Yeah, seventeen. Bigger than *me*, can you believe *that*?"

"And how's Marcy doin'?"

"You know Marcy, same old, same old, Jorge and her still goin' strong. They're a cute old couple now."

"Mm-hmm. Still never married."

"Marcy's never gettin' married. She said she would get married by the time she was seventy, remember?"

"Doesn't look like that's gonna happen. Hey Sam, the reason I called, was, uh... well..."

"What?"

"It's hard for me to say."

Bennett's voice cracked, feeling as though he was being run over by a defensive tackle, his chest laden with pressure, his heart jumping in and out of rhythm.

"I found out I have stage four heart disease, Sam."

Silence.

"What?! You're kidding, right?"

"Nope. Learned about it yesterday morning."

"My goodness... I dunno what to say. I'm—I'm shocked. That's terrible."

"Yeah, I figured I should let you and the others know."

"Have you told Marcy? Gene and Sophie?"

"Not yet. Nobody answers my calls."

"They're probably just busy. You know," Sam continued, "I talked to Gene a few weeks ago. It's nearly impossible to get ahold of him over there."

"You did?"

"Yeah, I've been trying to see if he'll be able to come home for Thanksgiving next month. You know you're welcome to come too, Ben..."

"Eugene might come home for Thanksgiving?"

"Well, he mentioned that he wanted to last time I talked to him."

"Where ya havin' it? At Marcy's house?"

"Yeah, Lucia won't be there this year either. I guess her and Mike are going to Europe for their anniversary, won't be back in time."

"What is that, twenty years for them?"

"Yeah. Thanksgiving though, will you think about it at least? I'd love to see you."

Bennett began to relax a bit. Then his phone vibrated. He looked at the screen. "Hey Sam, looks like Marcy's callin', I gotta let you go. But thanks, I *will* think about it. I'd love to see you guys too. It's been a long

[57]

time."

"Too long, brother. Alright, keep in touch. I'll be praying for you. Maybe this is a wake-up call?"

"Sure, Sam." Sam can't help himself, he thought. "I'll talk to you later." He switched over to Marcy on the other line. "Marcy?"

The signal battled poor reception. "Ben-ett? —nett, you there?"

"Yeah, I'm here!" Bennett strained. "Can you hear me?"

"Barely, t– phone re–pt— isn't ver- –od -ut here."

"What? The static is..."

"H-ld -n, — me –y – go ou–ide."

"Marcy, I can't understand a word you're saying!" He glanced at Mya. "God, that's horrible."

"Bennett? Do you hear me now?"

"That's much better."

"I don't get good reception at Jorge's. I had to step outside. So how's life for the prodigal son? Still living it up out there?" She was oftentimes rather facetious. It was one of her trademarks among other things he didn't much care for.

"Yep," he answered. "Still snortin' blow and bangin' out whores. That is, when I'm not burnin' crosses on lawns."

"Uh-huh. What did you call for? You never call."

"Marcy, cut it out. Christ, what's wrong with you? Can't your brother simply call every once and a while to say hello?"

"Um, excuse me but it was *you* who stopped returning *my* calls."

"Yeah! Because you can be overbearing! Like right now!"

[58]

"Overbearing? Is that what you called to tell me?"

"You know what, forget it."

"Okay, okay, go ahead. What's going on?"

He wasn't in the mood to talk to her anymore. "Well, uh, I thought you should know that..." Once again his words failed him. "I, um... I have..."

"Spit it out already."

"I have heart disease. *It's bad*. Stage four."

"Yeah, right." Marcy hadn't anticipated hearing anything like that and she didn't know what else to say. Insensitivity was another one of her unappealing trademarks. "Are you messing with me?"

"No, I'm not *messing* with you."

"Wow... I always said the chickens would come home to roost..." Marcy hesitated, not understanding why she'd said it.

"Seriously—"

"I'm sorry. That wasn't called for. I—I'm stunned. God! I can be an old bitch sometimes!"

"Jesus, yeah, ya think? How about a little fuckin' support? How about, 'Gee, Bennett, that's terrible. Is there anything I can do for you as your big sister?' Fuckin' A, does everyone in our family have to always sit on their goddamn high horse like they're leading the charge for the goddamn Almighty?"

"Shit. Um, I'm sorry, you're right. That was wrong of me. Is there anything I can do for you?"

"No, *not really*." He was about ready to hang up the phone.

[59]

"Actually, yeah. Sam says you're hosting Thanksgiving dinner this year? And that Lucia won't—"

"Wait, you don't mean—all these years—you're actually considering coming back?!"

"I'm considering it..."

"Well, Lucia won't be here. She and Mike are going to Europe, lucky them. I think that'd be terrific if you came down."

"If Sophia doesn't let me stay with her, will you—"

"Yeah, that's fine, you can stay with me. How exciting! I might get to see my brother and he's not even gonna make us fly all the way *out there* this time!"

"Yeah... We'll see..."

"Look, again, I'm *really* sorry. I feel like a jerk."

"Good, you *should* feel like a jerk. Anyway, Marcy, I gotta go. I just wanted to tell you that."

"Alright then, take care, Ben. Let me know what you plan to do. Call anytime, I mean it. I'll be praying for you."

"I'm sure it can't hurt. You too."

He hung up, his blood pressure receding to normal levels. Overall, the calls had gone pretty well. It was nice hearing about his nephews, Sam Jr. and Jimmy. He lit a cigarette and walked into his bedroom, opening his closet. He pulled out a box from the top shelf and brought it back to his recliner. Inside were the letters and photographs his son had sent from abroad over the years. The pile of photos consisted mostly of different fish, others of locations his tours had taken him to.

[60]

Eugene was an avid fisherman, having been taught by Mike, Lucia's boyfriend (now husband) after Bennett moved to Detroit. Melancholia filled him as he looked at the various mackerel, salmon, and sea bass. His son even caught an octopus once. That picture cheered him up a bit. Mya purred as he stroked her neck and scratched her ears, his mental reel rewinding to Christmas, 2000. He saw himself at Telly's, a small diner in Ferndale, smoking a cigarette, sipping coffee, Eugene sitting across from him.

"You know, dad," Eugene said, "you should really quit. My friend Jared, his mom—"

"Don't worry about me," he said with a grin, puffing on a Marlboro. "I'm as healthy as a horse."

"She died from lung cancer. Lifelong smoker."

"Yeah, that's awful... But I'm not ready to quit yet."

A waitress passed by with a pot of coffee.

"No thanks, I'm good," Bennett said, reverting his attention back to Eugene. "So tell me about the Navy. You're sure that's what you wanna do?"

"Yeah, I'm sure, dad. I'll fly out of Houston on the eleventh. Training is in North Chicago. I'll do that for eight weeks and then I'll find out where they're gonna station me."

"I'm glad you at least tried out Lone Star. College isn't for everyone, wasn't for me. How's your mom dealin' with it?"

"You know *mom*. She's worried, of course, especially since the USS

[61]

Cole."

"Yeah, that was sickening. Somethin' like seventeen sailors killed."

"Another forty injured. But you know, the group that did it, Al-Qaeda, they're a bunch of stupid shits, nothing but nomadic sand niggers incapable of mounting anything substantial. Small-scale bombings, that's all they do, like the ones on the embassies. They even blow themselves up, crazy motherfuckers."

A Middle-Eastern couple sitting nearby gave Bennett and Eugene dirty looks.

"Eugene, you can't say that here. Jesus, this isn't The Woodlands."

"What, 'crazy motherfuckers?'"

"No, sand ni—I'm not even going to repeat it."

"Sand nigger? Christ, dad, have you seen how those people live? They throw acid on girls' faces if they read books!"

"But Gene, remember, you're talking about a specific radical group. Most of them aren't like that. There's a lot of Middle-Easterners around here, they're quite nice actually."

"Jared, he's stationed in the Gulf right now," Eugene said, staring back at the couple with growing intensity in his voice, "and when his girl came to visit they went to Saudi Arabia, said they're like totally nuts over there. Women aren't even allowed to *drive cars*. Even so-called moderate Muslims believe blasphemy should be punishable by death. I mean, c'mon, really?"

"You know, women didn't have many rights in America a hundred years ago. Couldn't even vote. So they're slowly catchin' up.

They'll get there. You know what a lot of it is?"

Eugene sighed. "Yeah, yeah... *Religion*, the root of all evils, I know."

"No, I think irrational belief held beyond a reasonable doubt tends to be a *root cause* of evil because it fosters gullibility. That doesn't apply to religion exclusively and that doesn't make all religious *people* bad. It simply renders that type of mind more susceptible to nefarious thinking."

His imagination fast-forwarded a few years as he sifted through the letters, recalling the evening he was in the kitchen chopping carrots and saw that name flash across the TV: Jared Wagner. Jared, always twenty-four years old, the sting of another premature loss ripping through the world. Weeks later a post card arrived, dated June 16, 2006, the Spiral of Samarra on the front. Details of his death were scribbled on the backside. Eugene lost a few friends during Operation Iraqi Freedom but none as close as Jared. Helicopter crash over the Gulf, the note despaired. Investigators alleged it was mechanical failure. It was sent when Eugene was stationed in the region, hell's bottom, in the heat of war.

Bennett's head circled back to present reality, sitting in his apartment, despondent, Mya resting her head on his knee. Isolation crept over his being like frost on a sheet of glass. He missed his son and daughter. He looked at his cell phone. No missed calls. He picked Mya up, carried her off to bed, and fell asleep. His phone rang on the arm of the recliner where he left it.

The neurons in Bennett's brain transported his thoughts from his bed in Ferndale, Michigan to somewhere in the Pacific. The lucid dream had taken him aboard the USS Cole. He found himself asking every sailor he met if they had seen his son but each person walked by without paying him any notice. He floated through a door and stumbled upon a lavish cabin with a large bed in the center, a kitchen to the right side, and opposite to that a long table hosting an array of wine bottles. This must be the commander's bedroom, he figured. As he stepped closer to the bed he realized there was a woman underneath the blankets. She arose from the covers, unveiling a nipple and frazzled blonde hair. It was Angel.

"Where've you been, darling? Momma's been waiting for you."

"I, um, was over—uh," he fumbled, embarrassed that he forgot to close the door behind him.

"Don't worry about it sweetie. Come give momma some love."

He undressed and started making love to her. Angel rolled over so that she was on top of him, moaning, her facial expression bearing an uncanny resemblance to his ex-wife. His focus momentarily shifted to the door of the cabin where sailors casually passed without noticing the sex romp. Turning back towards Angel, her countenance changed as her voice morphed into belligerent rage. He instantly became petrified. The person before him was Lucia.

"You bastard! How the fuck could you?!" She jumped off him and began dressing herself.

Trying to explain himself, he mentioned his weaknesses, his overall dissatisfaction with life, even vowed to give marriage counseling a second go.

"It's over, Bennett! You're a fucking asshole! *Still* seeing that whore!"

He then scolded her for not paying enough attention to him, not understanding the stresses he had to deal with.

"Do you realize how much fuckin' money I've lost? That company in Tomball, they took everything! They got all the important contracts! Everywhere I go people say, 'Oh, I'd rather do business with that company that makes the military medals,' like it makes 'em feel fuckin' patriotic or somethin'!"

"Let me guess," she said, buttoning up her shirt, "it was *all* politics."

"Precisely!"

"It has nothing to do with that! Planck Awards is successful because they know how to do business. What do you do? You drink! You screw college whores!"

"That's fuckin' bullshit! They've been kickin' my ass for years now! It's because Joe fucked us!"

"Don't be ridiculous! Joe worked for the Guard. He had nothing to do with it!"

"To hell he didn't! He didn't tell me about it! And then the contract went to his buddies in—in—that other company!"

"Joe was trying to call you for days. Are you going to blame it on the birth of your son again? Is it your son's fault for being born that day

[65]

when Joe needed a definitive answer from you?" She finished putting her jewelry on, her eyes swollen with disgust. "Bennett, all you do is blame other people! You need to get your heart right with God, take some fucking responsibility! And don't tell me you're going through a mid-life crisis because you're too young for that!" She walked towards the door where a man stood. It was Mike, the man she would go on to marry.

Bennett examined them, confused. "What the hell is he doing here?"

She put her arms around Mike, kissed him, and then looked at Bennett with a wink. "He's taking me to Paris for our anniversary."

Before he had time to respond, an earsplitting blast shook the cabin, rocking everyone off their feet. Overcome with panic and a sort of ringing sensation in his ears, he glanced up to see Mike and Lucia quickly disappear into a crowd of sailors running to and fro past the door. His heart leapt while his muscles stiffened, unable to apprehend what was happening. Suddenly, his children came running into the room.

"Dad!" Eugene shouted, "We're under attack! Those sand niggers got us!"

"Have you seen your mother?" Eugene ignored the question, motioning him to follow. He tried to get up but perceived it difficult. He pulled himself up on the bed post and followed Eugene and Sophia through the ship's crowded corridors, scurrying through the madness up a number of staircases, the corridors getting smaller and smaller the further they ascended. He didn't exactly scurry per se. He never actually felt like he traveled on foot in his dreams. It was more akin to floating, though not once did it occur to him to examine his feet while moving about. He floated into a dark cellar, the surrounding noise growing fainter until he could no longer discern any distress.

"Eugene?" he called into the darkness which now completely engulfed him. "Sophia?" He couldn't see anything and nobody responded. He took a few steps forward and lost his balance, plunging into empty space. He kept falling for what seemed like minutes, screaming to the extent that he could, his heart in his throat, his lungs unable to catch a breath. At any moment he knew death would subdue him.

And then he woke up. He was on the floor next to his bed, gasping for air. He pounded his fist into the carpet, coughing relentlessly, sweat dripping off his forehead. He stumbled into his living room, unable to find the light switch, lit only by the moon which cast eerie shadows on his apartment walls. Mya was startled and ran off into a corner. He went to his bookshelf and grabbed a book he had bought a few months back but never opened. *The Interpretation of Dreams* by Sigmund Freud. His body shook, still unconvinced that the threat of war had only been in his head, his dream too vivid. With the book in hand, he plopped down in his recliner where his inhaler sat, regaining his equilibrium, never making it past the title page. The sound of rain steadily beating on his window began to sooth his nerves. He yawned, the clock on his microwave reading 2:35 A.M., lit a cigarette, and opened the window. He peered out into the parking lot and could hear through the showers a ukulele from Sara's apartment below him. He sat back down, deciding he would listen to her play along with the rain until he grew drowsy again. The scent of incense tickled his nostrils.

"You know what that is," he said to Mya, who slowly came out from hiding. "That's that incense daddy likes. That's Dragon's Blood."

VI.

A meaning of life

The sun briefly advanced above the horizon before retreating behind a coterie of rain clouds that loomed as far as the eye could see. Saturday's forecast called for showers throughout the day. The outside world carried on undeterred, birds singing from their shelter beneath drenched branches, feet shuffling up and down the streets under rain coats and umbrellas, everyone doing their best to avoid the puddles. Sara relaxed in her apartment with a cup of coffee, reading and painting, wondering when Bennett would come by to do art therapy with her. Shortly after noon it occurred to her that they had not settled on a time.

"Should I go knock on his door?" she thought aloud. "Nah, he's probably still sleeping, don't bother him."

Her boyfriend came out of the bathroom, dressing for work, fixed in one of his characteristically unpleasant moods. "We're still going to the show with Dominic and Abby tonight, right?" he asked.

"What show?"

"That new Scorsese one. Christ, I've mentioned it like three times this week."

"Hey, don't get that attitude with me. I haven't done shit to you this morning."

The two went back and forth until it escalated into one of their all too frequent arguments. He kissed her halfheartedly on his way out before slamming the door.

"God fucking damn him!"

Now alone in her apartment, she returned to her book on the couch, smoking her bong and listening to the downpour. Her eyes scanned the pages of *Siddhartha* but her thoughts trotted off somewhere distant and serene. All she could think was how she yearned to escape her current life, quit her job, school, go on the road somewhere and never have to deal with grumpy boyfriends or sit around and mope in her cramped apartment. Sara wasn't materialistic but every once in a while she would fantasize about living in an elegant Victorian mansion with chestnut floors and an assortment of hallways and rooms where one could easily get lost. One of the people she envied most was Sarah Winchester, the eccentric widow who built the marvelously absurd Winchester Mystery House in San Jose. That was the kind of house she dreamt of living in.

She took her mind off the present circumstances by pulling out her touch pad and watching silly videos on the internet: homemade footage of amateur daredevils performing idiotic stunts for no other reason than boredom. As she sat on her couch giggling at humanity's failures, she saw from the corner of her eye a man running outside in the rain with a leather jacket pulled over his head. It was Bennett, returning from his mailbox, a stash of envelopes and grocery ads

[70]

clutched to his hip. She opened up her front door as he was making his way up the stairs to his apartment.

"Hey Bennett!"

He looked down. "Oh, hello Sara."

"I was thinking about you a moment ago. Did you still want to...." She immediately became self-conscious of how desperate and lonely she sounded. He could sense it too, which prompted him to accept the invitation even though he wasn't exactly in the mood.

"Do a painting? Sure, okay. I'll be right down."

She went back inside and prepared her new brushes and paint tubes, placing a large canvas on her easel. A minute later Bennett knocked and proceeded to walk into her apartment, cigarette in mouth.

"May I?"

She nodded. "Can I have one?"

"Yeah?" he asked, surprised. "I didn't know you smoked."

"I don't but I need one right now. My boyfriend's been driving me crazy today. What do you smoke?"

He tossed her the box.

"Marlboro Special Blend... 100's?"

"What's wrong with that?"

"I never knew a guy who smoked 100's, that's all."

"Well, ya do now. I never understood why people think it's strange that I smoke 100's. I mean, you get more tobacco out of each one and they're the same price as regular cigs."

"Longer filter," she said, lighting up.

"Yeah but there's still more tobacco. Oh, guess what."

She invited him to sit down. "What?"

"I talked to my daughter this morning for two hours. That's a lot for me, I'm not much of a phone person."

"Oh, that's great! How did it go?"

"I'd say it went pretty well. We mostly chatted about small shit, which I enjoyed because we don't ever really do that. And we talked about some of our past issues, things she's resented me for. That was a little rough. She's still pretty angry with me. I told her about my heart, of course. Also, I talked to my brother and sister yesterday and I'm thinking about going down there next month for Thanksgiving."

"To Texas? Well, that's good to hear, Bennett. I'm happy for you. And they weren't all preachy and judgmental?"

"No, they were. Especially my daughter. I told her about the dreams I've been having lately and—"

"Dreams?"

"Yeah. Well, my whole life I've had these evocative dreams, recurring ones. They used to ruin my sleep but I grew pretty used to 'em. But lately, they've been especially intriguing, like blunders from my past cropping up, all mixed together, haunting me, like I still can't let go of 'em or somethin'."

"Mm-hmm. And what did your daughter say about it?"

"Ah, god, she thinks they're messages from the Lord, like 'Jesus is tryin' to soften my heart,' those were her exact words. She said I have

[72]

'unrepented sin.'"

"Do you?"

"You're kidding, right?" he chuckled, coughing out smoke.

"I don't mean in terms of the Christian guilt baloney but I mean do you have things you need to make right? People you've wronged?"

He paused and gave her a funny look. "Look kid, I'm sixty-two years old. Of course there are people I've wronged. Should I go look 'em up in the yellow pages and spend my last months on an apology tour searchin' 'em out?"

"Yellow pages? Uh, I think you mean the internet, old man. I don't mean to butt into your business but my father abandoned me when I was young—"

He grew stern. "I didn't *abandon* my children. My wife and I grew apart. She moved on with her life, I moved on with mine. I wanted to stay involved in their lives but she made it difficult. She put lies in their heads, made me out to be a terrible person when I wasn't."

"Maybe your daughter doesn't see it like that. You said yourself that you left them, that's all I'm sayin', I didn't mean to insinuate—"

"I'm sure. Listen, I've never claimed to be a saint. People fuck up, make mistakes. It's part of life. There are no magic words to change that. Nothing I can say will heal the hurt I've caused them overnight. I'm surprised we even talked the way we did today. Usually, my daughter doesn't call me back. But now with this illness, it's like I've been given one last shot to make things right with her. If I go back to Texas, I've gotta hope I can do that. That's one of the only things

[73]

keepin' me goin'."

"I understand." She got up, took a deep breath, and went to her French press. "Want some?"

"Sure."

She sat him down at the canvas and told him not to think about what to paint but to instead focus on everything he was going through, to let his subconscious move his hand, let the paint brush speak for him. He was cynical, insisting that his abilities as a painter were embarrassing, but she ignored his doubts, encouraging him onward.

"Can you light some of that incense you were burning last night? I could smell it from my window."

She held up a box of Dragon's Blood. "This?"

He nodded. The aroma filled the room while rain hammered against the pavement outside. Sara watched her aged student from the couch where she resumed her book, feeling contentment. The clocked ticked along. Five minutes later, Bennett stood up.

"I'm done," he proclaimed.

"That was fast." She walked over to the canvas, staring at a black space he had painted. "Hmm. Does it represent... Death?"

He lit another cigarette, smirking, coughing. "No, that's not *death*. That's every person who's ever lived, every thought ever conceived; every dream left unfulfilled, every pain endured. That's where Aristotle died, where Jesus died, George Washington died, and where *you'll* die someday. It's *life*."

"Alright," she said, still not understanding.

He pointed to a white dot near the center, too miniscule for her to have noticed. "See, that's the Earth as observed from Mars. An insignificant rock in the middle of an immense, pointless void. That's you and I right there."

"That's very perceptive, Bennett, but how about we try another? Maybe spend a little more time with it? Not that this one isn't good or anything but I dunno, put a bit more effort into it perhaps?"

He threw up his hands. "Well, what the hell! I thought the whole point was to *not* put any effort into it!" He could tell by the expression on her face she was not amused. "Okay," he said, "let me try one more. I'll do it over this one. But can we smoke some weed first?"

They got baked out of their wits and then he returned to the paint brush. He painted the curvature of a large sun at the top of one corner and a small circle which he colored to look like earth in the bottom corner opposite of it. The rest of the canvas he colored yellow and gray and placed a large black tree sprouting on earth, its roots consuming the humble planet, its width expanding the closer it reached his fiery sun. Dozens of branches extended from the ever growing trunk, twisted and pointed like those on a dead thorn bush. More branches extended from those and so on until there were tiny branches attached to increasingly larger ones, connected to the enormous trunk that all but disappeared at the bottom where its roots attached it to earth. He filled the space surrounding the sun, planet, and tree with swirls of navy blue and little silver dots to represent clusters of stars. On the very top of the tree he constructed two deformed branches that looked like

[75]

horns, placing two scarcely visible, dreary eyes below. The tree appeared to be half demon.

"I'm almost done," he said to Sara, who fiddled with her ukulele.

"Great!"

He glanced at the clock. He'd been painting for over an hour! "Wow, time flew by," he said, putting the finishing touches on his creation. "Alright, that—that about—does it." He got up, swelling with a sense of accomplishment.

Her jaw dropped when she saw his painting. "Bennett, that's magnificent... I'm impressed! And you tried to tell me you couldn't paint!"

His face turned red at the praise she heaped upon him.

"The tree looks frightening! What does this mean to you?"

He took a step backward and folded his arms, stroking his chin like an artist at the Louvre. "I guess the sun symbolizes what one might call 'Ultimate Concerns.' It's that essence, truth, purpose, or whatever it is we all strive for deep down in the marrow of our beings. The tree, of course, represents all life, that devil we call our humanity and the lesser evolved creatures we're connected with through DNA. We reach up to the sun only to find ourselves burnt by its heat when we get too close. Right when we think we've put on our finger on it, it kills us anyway. And uh, yeah, I think that's pretty much it."

"Hmm, okay," she said. "Does it feel good to have put that out there, on paper?"

"Yeah, you know what, it *does* feel good. I think it's the answer to

[76]

your question yesterday."

"Which was what?"

"Could I ever satisfy my search for meaning? Can man satisfy his innate desire to know, to mean something?"

"And?"

"No, he can't. And that's the point. I'm alive now and *that* is *a* meaning of life. There isn't only one meaning, there are many meanings, and *life* is one of them."

She concurred. "You know, Bennett, I think you might be onto something."

VII.

Shiva and Darwin

The remainder of Bennett's day was uneventful. He retreated into his apartment and continued reading *The Selfish Gene*, coughed up a storm while managing (barely) to smoke his pack of 100's, listened to the rain which periodically ceased then resumed; combed Mya's fur, ate leftover Parmesan Alfredo, ignored phone calls from acquaintances who wanted to know his Sunday plans, watched stupid television, and fell asleep in bed—all before midnight.

He woke up Sunday morning feeling refreshed. If he'd had any dreams during the night, he didn't remember them. This put him in an agreeable mood though it wouldn't last long. He drove his 2010 Mercury (one of the last Ford manufactured) up to the bank to withdraw some cash, then to the corner store to buy a case of beer. The sun radiated in the clear October sky, blades of wet grass dried, puddles on the sidewalk dissipated. His plan for the day was to get drunk and watch football. Today the Texans were hosting the Lions. He was rooting for Houston.

He bought his light beer, climbed back into his car, and began exiting the parking lot. Reverse lights from an SUV leaving another spot accelerated towards him, unaware his car was directly in its path.

"Goddammit," he said, sparing no time to catch the other driver's attention. He slammed on his horn but it was too late. The SUV smashed into his passenger side fender.

"Fuck me!" He put his car in park and stepped out to assess the damage. The other driver exited the SUV, a young black man, nineteen or twenty, Bennett guessed, tall and slender.

"I'm really sorry, sir," he apologized emphatically. "I didn't even see you coming."

Bennett's fender was cracked but beyond that there was minimal harm done. Still, it sent his blood pressure skyrocketing, his heart pounding in vexation. He was pissed.

"Yeah, obviously. Jesus *fucking* Christ, what're ya doin'? Weren't'cha lookin'?"

"I was but you came outta nowhere! Look, can we please not report this? This ain't even my car! It's my ma's!"

"Shit, it definitely wasn't my fault!" Bennett snapped, working himself into a frenzy. "I think I want to file a police rep—" Without warning, his chest seized up and he slipped into a coughing fit, hunching over his car before his knees caved into the cement.

"Fuck, are you alright?" the young man asked.

Bennett gasped for air, searching his pockets for his inhaler. After a brief moment, he located it and regained his composure, turning back towards the man who stared in distress. Bennett immediately broke out into laughter, again hunching over the side of his car to keep from falling over, tickled so hard he was almost in tears. The man was convinced Bennett was psychotic.

"Ha ha, oh Christ. I'll tell you what," Bennett said, attempting to maintain a semblance of sanity, "show me what you got in your wallet."

The man hesitated, mystified.

"C'mon," Bennett urged on, "I know you're not driving without a license 'cause then we'd have a much *bigger* problem on our hands."

He reached for his wallet and pulled it out.

"Open it up. How much money ya got?"

"I—I got thirty-six dollars, sir. See?" The man held his wallet out for Bennett to verify.

"Alright," Bennett continued, "by the way, what's your name?"

"Uh, Leon, s—sir."

"Leon, I'm Bennett." He extended his hand in greeting.

Leon nervously reciprocated.

"Here's what we're gonna do. You give me that thirty-six bucks so I can get my shit fixed and we'll call it even. The cops will never have to know about this."

Leon agreed, eager to see the matter resolved. He handed Bennett the money.

"*There* you go. Watch what the fuck you're doin' next time." Bennett turned to leave, then stopped. "On second thought, you know what, Leon? I'll keep this twenty, you take the rest and go make someone's day with it. Give it to someone in need, like a homeless person. Buy 'em lunch or somethin'. Can you do that for me, Leon?"

Leon remained baffled. "Oh, uh—sure—okay, no problem."

[80]

Bennett returned sixteen dollars, got back into his car, and drove off. That was that.

He arrived home and carried the case of beer up the stairs to his apartment, weighing the events that had preceded at the corner store. Bennett, what the hell is wrong with you? You didn't need that kid's money. You don't give a rat's ass about that car. You're gonna be dead in a couple of months anyway! Jesus, get a grip! He opened his door and took a seat at his café table. Mya meowed obsessively, pawing his leg.

"What do you want?" he snarled. "I already fed ya, Mya, now leave me the fuck alone already!" Mya tried to say "What the hell has gotten into you today?" in cat but it wouldn't come out right so instead she darted off to his bedroom.

He opened the case and resorted to his recliner, the early game minutes away from kick off. His phone vibrated in his pocket. He took it out and saw a text message from Marty. Marty was one of the guys he would regularly meet on Tuesday nights for poker, a friend he'd made many years earlier when he worked at the mortgage firm. "Why don't u answer ur calls?" it read. "@ Tesla's with Jackie and Tim for drinks + game." He set the phone on the arm of his chair; he didn't feel like going out to the bar, much less calling anyone back. Drained and uninspired, he figured he'd probably skip Tuesday night poker as well. Whatever trick Sara performed with that art therapy, he ruminated, its effects were long gone now.

[81]

By the end of the Houston-Detroit game, he was twelve and a half beers in. Mya slept across the headrest of his recliner, her furry tail resting upon his balding head like a toupee.

"The one game the Lions decide to win," he muttered, his words beginning to slur. He stood up and almost stumbled over. He had a decent buzz going. "Damn, I forgot cigarettes. I gotta go back to the store, Mya." He reached for his keys on the kitchen counter, knocking over half a dozen empty cans that sat there, tripping over his feet as he made his way to the door. He staggered downstairs and through the parking lot to his car, got in and fiddled with his keys, unable to fit them into the ignition. He slouched over the steering wheel and blacked out.

Sometime later in the afternoon, he was awakened by a knock on his window. Alarmed and dazed, he looked up to his left and saw a police officer motioning for him to open the door. "Ugh," he moaned, his head throbbing, his senses reactivated.

"You alright there, buddy?" the officer asked.

"Uh, yeah, officer," Bennett said, stepping to the side of his car, trying to gather his thoughts. "I fell asleep... by accident."

The officer scanned him suspiciously. "By accident, huh? We got a call that you've just been sittin' here. *You live here?*"

Bennett pointed to his apartment, the alcohol on his breath clinging to the officer's nostrils. "Yeah, right over there."

"You been drinkin' today?"

"No, sir—uh—well actually, yeah, a bit earlier."

"Did'ja drive? Did'ja come from somewhere or..."

"No, no, I live here. I simply came out to, uh, look for my cigarettes, and then I—well, I fell asleep."

"Uh-huh, I'm gonna have to see some identification."

Bennett reached into his back pocket. "Shit, ya know what, my I.D. is in my apartment."

"What apartment did you say?"

"Twenty-two. That one, right *there*."

"Alright, I'll tell ya what," the officer said, "you go on home. *I'm gonna let you off with a warnin'.* I could cite you for public intoxication so keep the drinkin' inside, you understand?"

"Yes, officer."

The officer watched as he hurried back to his apartment, uttering profanities under his breath: "Public intoxication my ass. I fuckin' live here... gonna let me off, sure... try to arrest me, goddamn pig."

He resumed drinking once he got inside, watching the rest of the day's games, still fiending for a cigarette. When they concluded he looked at his watch and remembered that tomorrow was Monday, which meant he was expected to return to work, which in turn meant he would have to wake up by 5 A.M. to get to the shop by 6.

"I'm gonna have the worst hangover tomorrow," he told Mya as he wobbled off to bed.

Indeed he did.

Beep! Beep! Beep! Beep! He hit the snooze twice before attempting

[83]

to get out of bed.

"Ah, my fucking chest!" He tried to get up but weakness permeated his body, his chest feeling as though it held a rotting carcass inside, *himself* decaying. He could recall little from the dream he awoke from except that he was on a bus which drove off a bridge, plunging straight into deep, turbulent rapids. Kicking the glass out of the emergency door, he swam through the cold waters, rescuing passengers without a jot of fear. Aside from a few unknown faces, those he saved included his brother Sam, Sara, her boyfriend, and the young man from the corner store, Leon. He had no idea why he dreamt that he was on a bus with these people. The cop was also on board but he did not try to rescue him.

The more he thought about the dream, the less of it he remembered, a swash of mental images receding into the void. Nothing made sense to him this morning. He was going to a job for a paycheck that didn't matter anymore (his ten grand in the bank more than enough to last him a few months). When he approached Mya to greet her, she hissed. Even the shower mocked him, only doing the opposite of what he wanted, the knob for hot water spewing out cold, the knob for cold spewing out hot. The world appeared more egregious than usual. He waited impatiently in traffic as if it made the slightest difference whether he showed up at work on time or not, stopped to get cigarettes, and arrived ten minutes late, realizing he didn't care after all.

"Welcome back, Ben!"

"Feelin' better?"

"You had us all worried!"

"I knew you'd pull through!"

The congratulations, the consolations, *everyone* acknowledged him as he walked through the shop, and all of their words felt empty. Nobody knew what was *really* going on. He wondered if they only pretended to care, more joyful over the fact that they wouldn't have to cover his workload anymore.

"John wants to see you," Dave told him as he poured a cup of coffee in the break room. He went over to see his foreman.

John pointed to a large crate. "Hey bud, take a seat. How ya holdin' up?"

"Eh," he said, sitting down, gesturing mediocrity. "I've been better. It was difficult gettin' here this morning."

"The meds helpin' much? The blood thinner or whatever?"

"Yeah, that and some pills, they're doing what they're supposed to I guess."

"Do ya gotta go in for a follow-up or anything?"

"I dunno yet. Still gotta figure out my finances, not havin' insurance and what not."

"You don't qualify for Medicare yet?"

"Nah, a few more years still."

"You can't get *anything* through the government? Don't they fine you if you're not covered?"

"There aren't any good plans available for me. I figured it'd be cheaper to pay the fine 'til I turn sixty-five."

[85]

"You're probably regrettin' that now, eh?"

"Yep..."

"Well, welcome back. While you were gone I put Fred on your job and he hardly did shit. So, even though you probably wanna take things a *little easy* the next few days, I need ya to get things caught back up. And keep an eye on Dave and him."

"What for?"

"Do I really have to tell you, Ben? Because they're fucking morons!"

"Oh, right."

"Alright, now get to work."

He walked away and went to his machines, annoyed by John's sudden interest in his life. John rarely ever treated him kindly before the incident, before his heart attack. He was always criticizing him, telling him how slow and inefficient he was, how he should retire already or find something less strenuous to do. John was a fairly young man, in his late thirties, clean shaven, starting to bald. Bennett suspected that he no longer fucked his wife, which explained why he spent most nights at the bar sweet-talking younger, prettier girls whom he would also never fuck. He was the type of person whose misery was obvious to everyone but himself, stumbling upon his position of power the way most authority figures do: by kissing a lot of ass.

The machines Bennett worked on were rod mills. People brought him sheets and bars of steel from the heat furnace, after they went through various stands and cooled. He'd feed them through his machines to produce different sized rod coils, the main product the steel mill manufactured. If the bars were large enough, they'd get transported by a hi-low. He enjoyed driving the hi-lows but otherwise it was a mundane and relentless job. The only reason he'd worked there for so long was that the pay was decent and he was experienced in metalwork. The day lasted ten hours, from 6 A.M. to 4 P.M., minus a half hour break for lunch and two fifteen minute breaks, one in the morning and one in the afternoon.

He toiled through the first half of the day, smoking cigarettes, shooting the shit with Dave and Fred since they worked in the same vicinity. He thought about ditching the place and going home, his mind fixated on his illness and the allure of his warm, cozy bed. It took everything in him not to. After lunch, John came by for his ceremonial bitching as he did every day, inspecting each person to see how their jobs were going and to find something to yell about. John never missed a beat and today was no exception, even for Bennett.

"How's it comin', Ben?"

"Good," he answered, barely turning to acknowledge him.

"Ben, what's this crap all over the floor?"

"Just some scraps, John, I was gonna pick up 'em."

"Fuck yeah you were, pick 'em up *right now*. And I thought I told you to keep an eye on *those two*," he said firmly, glancing at Dave and Fred.

All Bennett heard from John's lips was "blah, blah, blah." He'd about had enough of him, of the steel mill, of taking orders. He looked over at Dave and Fred, who watched from afar, making sexual gestures behind John's back, then turned to John, his lips still moving, his brow contorted to demonstrate seriousness or something like that. He couldn't hear a word. It was as if space-time became stationary, sound waves incapable of traveling through his ear drums to his nerve cells. The moment came to a climax when Bennett finally spoke up, collapsing his current tunnel of reality, reconnecting him to the external world.

"John."

"Ben, are you listening to me?! What?!"

Bennett stood silent.

"Goddammit! *What?!*"

"Fuck off!" Bennett was not fully aware of what he was saying or what caused him to say it. "*I quit!*" He took the cigarette in his mouth and threw it on the floor, stomping it out, and marched off to his locker to clean out his things.

"Hey! You can't quit on me right now!" John yelled, his voice fading as Bennett walked away. "You walk outta here, Shepherd, and you're not comin' back! I'm serious! I don't care what's wrong with you!"

Bennett passed Dave and Fred, smiling proudly as they stared, stunned, both envious of what he had just done. His name became infamous at the mill for some time after that.

"Hey assholes, get back to work!" John screamed at them, his face resembling a pomegranate.

Bennett got into his car and started driving, his grin fading only after many miles. It was a sunny Monday afternoon, a perfect day to cruise around with the windows down, the breeze whisking over the few hairs left on his head. He didn't feel like returning home so instead he zipped past his exit, continuing east on the freeway towards his secret getaway about thirty miles northeast of Detroit.

When he arrived at the familiar destination, he parked his car and walked through a wooded trajectory until he came to the edge of Anchor Bay at Lake St. Clair. The site of autumn was breathtaking, richly colored leaves dangling from their branches like little corpses, the splendor of death in motion. He took about twenty steps to his left and found his sacred mound. His imagination carried him away to the distant past, summertime, 2004:

He stood on that same patch of grass and dirt hidden in the woods off Anchor Bay, his eyes swollen from weeping the entire ride there. It was a cloudy, sultry afternoon, a dog day.

"This looks like the spot, Shiva," he said, wrestling to keep his poise. He planted a shovel into the ground and began digging, his heart broken, his mind drowning in the pain of loss.

"I remember when Angel and I first saw you," he said, tossing dirt aside. "You were the most beautiful pup I ever saw. Angel wasn't sure about you, she didn't want a Greyhound but I convinced her." He wiped his eyes and looked over at the bundle of blankets on the grass close by. "You were the best dog a man could ever want. Angel came around. She wanted to take you so badly but I wouldn't let her. Five

[89]

years you stuck with me after she left. I got back on my feet like I promised you I would."

When he finished prodding the hole he stepped over to the blankets on the ground and knelt. He lifted the covering off Shiva's head and put his face into her dark brindle fur, kissing her and whispering his final farewell. He picked up the dead dog and placed her in the wooden box he'd built. Shiva was his favorite pet, he reflected. She lived a good life before succumbing to old age. He buried her in the spot where he now stood fourteen years older, chubbier, balder, jobless, and terminally ill.

His thoughts wandered forward from 2004 to the spring of 2013. That was the year he buried his flat-faced cat Charles Darwin, named after one of his idols, next to the spot where Shiva lay. He didn't have as many pleasant memories of Darwin, a black and brown Persian. He'd located him one night, then a small kitten, malnourished, deserted, crying in a dumpster. This was shortly before Shiva passed. He was adorable and a good fit at first, well-tempered, affectionate. As he grew older, however, he became anti-social and hostile, probably the result of abandonment issues, Bennett figured. Darwin was regularly plagued by ill-health, eventually dying of feline infectious peritonitis at the age of nine, otherwise known as the FIP virus. Bennett didn't shed nearly as many tears at Darwin's funeral though his heart ached nonetheless. He recalled how after Darwin died a former co-worker at the steel mill announced that he was selling kittens. That's how he came to acquire the orange long-haired tabby he named Mya. He thought she was a better cat than Darwin.

As he sat on a large rock in his sacred woods, smoking cigarettes, immersed in everything around him—the spectrum of colors, the calmness of the waters, the smell of fresh air—he began to contemplate the pets he'd owned over the years. He thought about the family dog, Ginger, from when he was a boy, the two Siamese cats he and Lucia once shared, Sade and Ralph, the other small animals he cared for in between: fish, lizards, turtles, and even mice. He truly loved life and that is what saddened him most in having to let it all go. It wasn't the idea of nothingness (which he was certain death entailed) that bothered him most; it was all of the simple joys, even amidst the sorrows, that he would no longer experience, the grandchildren he would never get to meet, the technologies he would never witness, the truths he would never discover. All of that depressed him, the vacuum of hopelessness nagging at whatever optimism he still claimed. Nevertheless, it was not a day for mourning. He needed to celebrate having freed himself from the steel mill. He walked back to his Mercury and drove toward home.

VIII.

The time is now

Bennett cruised along, flipping through radio stations, searching for something to listen to. None of the music appealed to him and he was tired of hearing the same albums in his collection. Instead, he settled on a talk radio program. He didn't realize it at first but he selected a Christian station. The host's name was Paul Fortier, the topic of today's program, Creationism vs. Evolution. This should be interesting, he thought sardonically.

"Okay, we're going to take some of your calls right after this break," Fortier said.

"Hi there listeners," an advertisement began, "this is Paul Fortier from The Paul Fortier Show and I want to tell you about a new product from Manna Industries called Transfiguration 7-X. Now folks, I'm sure if you're like me, always working, on the go, not getting enough sleep, you probably feel wiped out by the middle of the week. Not anymore. Transfiguration 7-X is a vitamin developed by the God-fearing scientists at Manna Industries. One vitamin each morning will literally transform your life. So please, I'm telling you folks, call 1-555-MAN-NA7X, that's 1-555-MAN-NA7X, and get your Transfiguration 7-X vitamins today. Start living up to your God-given potential."

Bennett couldn't help but mark the irony.

"Everything was going so wonderful," a distressed woman began, gloomy melodic notes from a piano in the background. "We were planning a trip to the Bahamas. One day it all changed. My husband George had a heart attack."

His ears perked up.

"It was so scary," she continued, "and even worse, our policy didn't cover the treatments George needed. We were going to have to sell our house and auction everything we owned to cover the costs! I thought our lives were over!" Then she became an idealist, though none the better actress. "That's when Craig Donaldson stepped in. Craig not only fought *for us* but *with us*, helped us secure a low-interest loan and found us the efficient, affordable medical care we *thought* our policy included. Now George is healthy, happy, and feeling himself again."

"Honey!" a man shouted in the distance. "C'mon, we're going to miss our flight!"

"We're going to the Bahamas," she giggled.

"Not protected?" asked a full-bodied, masculine voice. "Does your plan leave you vulnerable? Call the offices of Craig Donaldson and know your options. 1-555-208-4126. Don't choose between going broke and watching your loved one die, that's 1-555-208-4126, 1-555-208-4126."

Bennett searched his car for a pen, trying to retain the number in his short-term memory. "1-555-208-21 —" he said aloud. "No, it was 1-555-208-416—Shit." He forgot it.

"Hi folks," the returning host said. "The Paul Fortier Show is back

[93]

and I said I would get to your phone calls so we're gonna do that now starting with Keith in Roseville. Hello Keith, you're on The Paul Fortier Show."

"Hi Paul," the caller said. "I wanted to ask you about Genesis 1 where it says God created the heavens and the earth. Uh, how did God create them?"

"You mean like the process God used?" Fortier asked.

"Yeah," replied the caller. "My friend, a non-believer, asked me the other day how God created the Universe. I told her that God is God and can do anything, even speak things into existence. She told me that amounted to a non-answer, to basically saying 'I don't know.' I didn't know how to respond to that."

"Well, it didn't sound like a non-answer," Fortier chuckled, "but you're right, Keith, God *can* do anything because he is God! That means he is omnipotent, that is, all-powerful! And that's how he created the Universe. The Bible says, 'God said, "Let there be light," and there was light.' It says his ways are beyond our understanding. We can't know the exact process God used but we can certainly look forward to getting to heaven and asking God ourselves!"

Goodness, Bennett mused, *that's* a satisfactory explanation if there ever was one! God waved his magic wand, abracadabra, and the Big Bang happened! Now believe all this other nonsense I'm about to tell you! his internal cynic sneered.

"Okay, let's go to Patty in Sterling Heights," Fortier continued. "Hi Patty."

"Hi Paul, I wanted to comment on this liberal, atheist agenda we see being pushed onto our kids in school. My daughter came home yesterday and told me that her teacher said we descended from monkeys, and she stood up for the faith—"

"*Wonderful*," Fortier chimed in.

"Oh, I was *so* proud of her, Paul. She said she asked the teacher where morality comes from if we're all just monkeys and he couldn't give her an answer. But could you comment on that, the degradation of our culture, our values, and how it relates to this secularism, this godless way of thinking that's being shoved down our children's throats?"

"Sure, Patty. Notice how they don't even *allow* other viewpoints into the classroom and pretend that evolution is a fact, *which it is not*. I've often pointed out how Darwinism's gospel is survival of the fittest, how this leads to the eugenics of Nazi Germany, how—"

Bennett turned off the radio, unable to stomach any more. It bothered him to consider how many credulous listeners would take the host's unqualified statements as truth, but, he surmised, that's why Jesus called his followers sheep.

"Yeah," he deliberated aloud, "the fact that we evolved means we're incapable of distinguishing between actions that improve our lives and those that inflict unnecessary destruction and tragedy. I mean, really?" He thought about calling in and educating the radio host but didn't. From conversations he'd had with his family over the years, he saw it as pointless.

[95]

He got off the freeway a few exits before his and drove to a bar called The Showcase. He knew the bartender, a woman named Jasmine, having briefly dated a number of years back. He pulled up to the hole in the wall, the building practically unchanged throughout its forty-year history. The Showcase was a small rundown karaoke bar with a few booths, a billiards table, a dart board near the back, and a small dance floor where entertainment was sometimes presented. Usually vacant, he wondered how they managed to stay in business over the years. Inside were only two other patrons besides himself.

"Hey Jazz," he said as he sauntered up to a bar stool and sat down. Jazz is what everybody called her.

"Bennett! It's been a while since I've seen you in here."

"I know, too long. I've been busy with work and stuff lately. How're ya doin'? Things good here?"

"Yeah, slow as usual. I'm doin' good though. Katie's gettin' her driver's license in like three weeks."

"Wow, time sure does fly, doesn't it? They grow up so fast."

"Sure do. You know my birthday's coming up too? You probably don't remember."

"That's right, it is. You're gonna be—"

"Fifty," she said reminiscently. "I can hardly believe it."

"Hey, ya look great, I wouldn't have guessed. Doin' anything special for it?"

"Dinner with the family, nothing extravagant. Who wants to celebrate that?" she laughed.

[96]

"I hear ya. I suppose I'll have to get ya somethin'."

"Nah! So what can I get you today?"

"Um, I'll go with a Jack and coke, please."

"Sure thing," she said, turning around to fetch his drink.

Bennett meant it too. Jazz didn't look a day older than thirty-five. She was of Iranian descent, had long dark hair, a curvy but trim figure, wore tight jeans which he admired from the rear while she prepared his drink. She was into Wicca, dressed holistically, like a gypsy, regarded herself a part-time witch—that is, when she wasn't tending the bar.

She handed him a picture of her daughter. "That's her now."

Katie, whom he knew as a young girl when he and Jazz dated, strongly resembled her mother. "She must have inherited your genes. She's turning into a beautiful woman."

"Isn't she?" She set his drink on the bar. "So how's work going?"

"It's funny you should ask. I quit today."

She looked surprised. "At the steel mill? You worked there for what, ten years? What happened?"

He looked at his glass and sighed. "It was time to go."

"I don't understand."

"Wanna step outside for a minute?"

"Sure. Hey guys," she called out to the other two patrons, "do you need anything? I'm stepping outside for a smoke."

"We're good, Jazz!" they hollered back.

She stepped outside the back door where Bennett stood smoking.

[97]

He held out his box of Special Blends "Need one?"

"No, I got some. I don't smoke non-menthol anyway."

"Since when?"

"Got hooked on these Camel Menthols about a year ago. I don't know, maybe it's menopause. Tastes buds changed too. Never liked pumpkin pie, now I love the stuff. So what's up?"

"Look Jazz, I might as well tell you... I—uh—I have stage four congestive heart failure."

She gasped. "What?! What're you saying?"

"Doctor gave me a few months..."

She didn't believe him at first but once he explained how he collapsed at work, how he didn't have insurance, and how his emotions about it didn't really compute, she broke down in tears.

"Ah, Bennett, that's the worst thing I've heard!"

He tried to humor his friend. "Ever?"

"That I can remember! What're you going to do? You have to get treatment!"

"At this point, the doctor said I would need a transplant. It's not likely. Even if I had the money, there's a waiting list, ya know?"

"Have you told your kids?"

"I told Sophia. Haven't been able get in contact with Eugene but I hear he might be coming home for the holidays. I'm thinking about going down to Texas next month."

"Don't tell me you came to say your goodbyes, Bennett!"

"I'm sure I'll see you again before I go." He patted her on the back, doing his best to console her. "C'mon, you've got a bar to tend. Let's go back inside."

Devastated, she struggled to pull herself together.

"Jasmine, you're at work... Don't make a scene... Besides, I'm not dead yet!"

She wiped her eyes, trying to collect herself. "Dammit, Bennett... Alright."

He followed her back inside, finished his Jack and coke, and then departed.

He pulled into Willow Lane as the sun was beginning to set. "What a day!" he said to himself. Walking through the parking lot to his apartment, he noticed his cousin Jon in Virginia had left him a voicemail earlier. Even though Jon was younger than Bennett by eleven years, he was his favorite cousin, their association deeper than blood, endeared to one another by a shared disdain for the faith they were both raised in. Unlike his other family members, they maintained frequent contact. (A little background: Bennett's father was from Virginia, having moved to Texas where he met Bennett's mother in the '40s. Virginia is where most of Bennett's extended family lived. His father had been the black sheep of his family like Bennett was in his. Go figure. His mother had no siblings or close cousins. Jon's parents—*his* mother being Bennett's father's sister—were the only family members to visit the Shepherds in Texas.)

He started up his staircase, phone in-hand ready to call Jon, when at

[99]

that instant Sara's door swung open. He hadn't seen her since Saturday and stopped to see if she was leaving, wanting to say hello. Out of the door walked a young black man. It was Leon, the kid who backed into Bennett's fender the day before. The moment their eyes met, Leon jumped back, briefly convinced that Bennett was a hallucination (conversely, Bennett could tell that Leon was baked out of his mind, presumably from Sara's bong).

"Oh, hey," Sara said, walking out behind Leon. She appeared flustered.

"Hey Sara. Hi Leon."

"Do—do you two know each other?" she stuttered, unsure as to why Bennett and Leon stood motionless, staring at one another.

"Sara, this is the crazy dude I was tellin' you about! The one I hit yesterday with my ma's car!"

"Bennett?"

"Yeah! That's him! So you mean this is the guy dyin' from cancer or whatever?"

"It's congestive heart failure actually," Bennett asserted.

Leon looked at Bennett, his face scrunched up like a flat-faced cat, the kind Darwin had been. "If you're dying then why the hell did you take my money?"

Bennett shrugged. "It was the principle." He continued into his apartment. "I'll see you later, Sara."

He walked inside and greeted Mya, fed her a can of beef bits in gravy, then sat down in his recliner. He pulled out his phone, took a deep breath, his heart feeling uneasy, his nerves anxious, and dialed his cousin.

"Hey Ben!"

"Hey cuz, how're ya? I noticed you called."

Jon wasted no time getting straight to the point. "I talked to Sam yesterday... god, he—he told me the news. Weren't you gonna let me know, Ben?"

"Yeah, I was going to, Jon. I didn't get around to it. I haven't exactly wanted to talk about it a whole lot, know what I mean?"

"Shit's crazy. I still don't wanna believe it. Isn't that what—"

"Yep, same thing that killed my father."

"But he had your mom to deal with."

"Yeah. After mom went nuts, it took a toll on him. I think he felt guilty, and the stress too, it did him in. Hey, how's Aunt Jill and Uncle Ron?"

"They're good, you know my folks," Jon said. "Gonna be ninety soon and they're both still active, golfing, bingo—you name it—still livin' it up out in Pasadena."

"They really like it there, eh?"

"Oh yeah, pops loves it, says he wishes he would've left Virginia a lot sooner. So Ben, what's your plan?"

"The prognosis isn't good."

"Man, I'm so sorry..."

"What can ya do, ya know? I appreciate it."

"I just want to say, even though you guys haven't had the greatest relationship through the years, your family still cares a tremendous amount. I know you don't need to hear it from me but for *your* sake *and* theirs, work out your differences, the sooner, the better. Like I've always said, the time is now, right? I'm sure they're willing to help with anything... And of course, I'm always here for you too. By the way, I heard you might be goin' down there for Thanksgiving..."

Jon's right, Bennett thought, the time *is* now.

"...I'd love to meet up or something. As far as money—"

"No, no," Bennett said assuredly. "I've got some money saved up, I'll be fine. Yeah, that would be superb, maybe I can pass through on my way down to Houston."

"I hope you do. Well look, I gotta run but if there's anything I can do, don't hesitate to call. I'll check up on ya in a few days."

"Thanks, Jon."

"See ya."

Bennett hung up the phone, made a couple hamburgers, and watched TV for a while; first Monday night football, then the local news, then part of a comedy show that he didn't recognize or understand. He couldn't stop thinking about what Jon said, that little phrase continually looping in his brain, "the time *is* now." He imagined what life would be like if all numbers on clocks were replaced by simply the word *now*.

It grew late and he became tired. He got up, went into his room, and dozed off, dreaming that he was driving his car into Tomball, going full speed, swerving through traffic...

[102]

He pulled up to Melvin's Psychiatric Hospital, the psyche ward where his mother spent much of her life during her last five years. Police cars surrounded the front of the building. He raced to a parking spot and dashed from his car to the entrance where he found his father talking to officers inside the lobby, a complete mess, in a daze, rife with shock. His wife was there, as were his siblings. Marcy was in tears, Lucia trying to comfort her. The police told him another patient, for no apparent reason other than the fact that she regarded his mother annoying, bashed her head in with a telephone. The place was understaffed and nobody realized what was going on until his mother's head resembled mashed Spam and egg shells covered in tomato sauce.

Bennett's father kept repeating, "It was my fault. It was my fault."

"*How can you blame yourself?*" Sam asked. "You didn't do it!"

"I was too hard on Jack," their father mourned. "When he passed she lost her mind. If I wasn't so hard on him, he would have never gotten into that stuff and she would still—"

"Dad," Bennett tried to explain, "Jack had a drug problem, it wasn't your fault. Perhaps you were hard on him but you can't blame yourself for what he did or how mom reacted. Sometimes shit happens."

As he stood there observing his grieving family, he heard a frail voice whisper:

[103]

"Bennett."

His mother's ghostly figure stood behind him, covered in blood from head to toe, a thick red trail dripping from her gown onto the green and beige tiles covering the lobby floor.

"Have you talked to Jack lately, Bennett?"

"No, mom, he's dead. Jack is dead."

She shrieked as if in sudden agony.

"Bennett!" his father yelled, "What have I told you about upsetting your mother like that?! Can't you see she's already past her breaking point? She's going mad! She talks to herself! I had to get her on meds! Now shut the fuck up already!"

The nightmare grew more intense. Lucia came towards him, cursing, tears running down her cheeks.

"You fucking liar!" she yelled. "I called The Skipper Hotel! You checked in with that woman!"

"What?!"

"They sent a postcard, Bennett! To thank you for your overnight stay! I called 'em! How could you fucking do this to me?!" she cried. "You liar! Who the fuck is she?!"

"A postcard?! Please, let's talk about this!"

"Who the fuck is she?! Who *the fuck* is she?!"

Bennett hurled forward, panting, finding himself back in his room, in his bed, the night still relatively young. There were screams coming from the apartment below.

"Who the fuck is he?! Who *the fuck* is he?!"

Sara's boyfriend was shouting. The guy must have figured something out, probably something to do with that Leon kid, Bennett speculated. He'd heard Sara and her boyfriend argue frequently, even before he knew who she was, but they always seemed to quickly make up. This fight sounded different, worse than the others, objects clashing as if getting thrown around and broken. Sitting in bed, amused, annoyed, he tried to get back to sleep but to no avail. Eventually he heard Sara's front door slam and what sounded like a woman yelling outside, begging someone not to leave. He got up and looked out his window, regretting his decision the moment she turned around and saw him. Retreating to his bed, he wondered if he should check on her but determined it was none of his business. Some time passed and as his eyes lids began to sink, his thoughts gradually returning to the Land of Nod, there was a knock on his door.

"Kinda late to be knockin' on doors, don't'cha think?" he said to Sara upon seeing her in his entryway. She didn't appear well, her eyes puffy from crying.

I—I saw you in the window," she sniffled. "I can go if it's not a good time..."

He sensed her desperation. "No, no, now is always a good time. You okay? Wanna come in?"

"I brought a doobie," she said, holding it up. "I thought maybe

[105]

you'd wanna smoke with me. I could really use the company."

He stepped aside and motioned her in.

"Coffee?" he asked, putting her jacket on a stool and inviting to her to sit.

"Yes, please. I'm sorry if I woke you."

"It's no problem, it's only quarter to two anyway."

She couldn't tell if he was being sarcastic.

"You're going to be tired at work tomorrow, aren't you?" she asked. "You did go back to work today, right?"

"Yep." He lit a cigarette, leaning on the kitchen counter. "I went to work today and quit. Figured if I'm gonna die in a few months, I'm not spendin' any more time at a goddamn factory takin' orders from those sons of bitches."

She nodded her head, still sniffling. "You've actually seemed surprisingly calm through this whole ordeal."

"Eeyore, remember? Eeyore doesn't lose his shit. Break my heart and I might lose it, tell me I'm dyin' and I'll tell you to tell me somethin' I don't know."

He brought her a cup of coffee and sat down in his recliner, eyes fixated on the joint. "You gonna light that up? So what happened? Boyfriend catch ya two-timin' with the black kid?"

She lit the marijuana. "Leon?"

"Shit, that smells good... Mm-hmm. I'm not stupid, Sara. Guys know when somethin' is up."

"Okay, look, it was one time. He works with me, we hung out a couple of times, he kissed me, you know how that goes."

"*More than you know.* And then?"

She looked down at her lap where Mya had curled, disgusted with herself. "And then we slept together. I knew it was wrong, I felt terrible cheating on Tom. I told Leon today I couldn't see him like that anymore."

"Tom's your boyfriend? I don't think you ever told me his name."

"Yeah, well, *was*."

"You think it was a good idea to have Leon over to tell him that?"

"That's not why he was over. He was over to do art therapy."

"*Sure,*" Bennett chuckled.

"He was! His mom is havin' surgery this week, breast cancer, and he's been going through some shit, ya know? I told him to put it on paper."

"Mm-hmm. And you don't think Tom will come back *because...?*"

"Because Tom told me he's been seeing someone else too." She began to break down again. "I dunno what to do, Bennett, I've been depressed lately. It feels like I have nothing going for me, no purpose. I try my best to ignore it, reminding myself of all the beautiful things in the world, but ugliness somehow always overcomes it. I feel.... Alone."

"Hell, welcome to the Cosmos. The one thing I *do* claim to know is that it's completely *indifferent* to us. People don't seem to take that too well. I've lived alone for six years, it isn't *that* bad. You get used to it, learn to find the things that really please you, make you happy. Wait 'til you find out you're *dying*."

[107]

"No, you're right. It's just... Nothing brings me satisfaction anymore and I don't get it."

"C'mon, you're twenty-four! You've got time to figure it out! It's only a break up, you'll get over it. Maybe you'll discover that you're better off now."

She stared at the wall, too ashamed to look at him. "Tom and I dated for *four* years. Four! Tom was one of the few people I understood, who understood me... And he helped me a lot with money. I don't think I'll be able to go to school *and* live here. I'd have to go live with my mom in Hazel Park. I don't want to go back there."

"Sometimes you gotta make tough choices. What's so awful about your mom's?"

"Oh, don't even get me started. For one, she's an alcoholic. She's overbearing, gets me to do things for her simply because she can. She's manipulative. God, I love my mom but she's dreadful to be around when we live together. We don't get along, let me leave it at that."

"I can understand that."

He did his best to console her. They ended up talking until the morning, discussing her fortunes, his fate, her heartache, his heart disease, memories. She cried on his shoulder. He tried to cry but couldn't. His emotions still hadn't fully caught up with him; the animosity, at nature, his genes, at the fact that his life was being cut short, he couldn't bring it to the surface. It stayed bottled inside him like a time bomb.

His eyes began to burn from insomnia. Sara went home and he

stumbled into his room, falling over his bed, feeling a serene detachment. Sadness came and went in spurts, the anger controlled for now. He kept it together, repeating the same words in his head, telling himself that death wasn't real. Presently, he was alive.

"The time is now."

IX.

Longing

Bennett and Mya slept through most of the next day. He dreamt many bizarre ideas, some relating to past experiences left strongly impressed on him, others ostensibly meaningless. Only one of these did he recall when he woke up, however. It was a memory about his first love as a boy, Sally James.

Sally grew up with Bennett in Tomball. She went to the same school, kept the same friends. Moreover, her father had been the minister at Calvary Church, where the Shepherds attended every Sunday. Though Bennett sang the words during service, his concern was fixed on the choir, an all-girl group made up of the 12 to 16-year-olds, which included Sally. The sequence in which he found himself was the night he tried to kiss her. In reality, it took him months of self-encouragement to finally work up to this moment. Lingering on a park jungle gym, the sun waning in the horizon, he made his move and leaned in...

"I—I'm sorry we couldn't talk yesterday," she said, drawing her head away, her eyes glued to the ground. "I had homework, I—I—my dad wouldn't let me use the phone..."

"Aw, it's alright."

He wrapped his arm around her, pulling her closer, determined to taste the interior of a girl's mouth for the first time. His lips eased forward...

Suddenly, her legs began shaking.

"What the...?"

Without saying a word, she pushed him off and ran home in tears.

When he woke up on Tuesday afternoon, October 16, 2018, in Ferndale, Michigan—as opposed to Tomball, Texas, spring of 1971— he felt emotionally drained. He remained in bed wondering why he dreamt of Sally James after not having thought of her in decades, reflecting on everything that transpired after that evening in the park so many years ago, struck by the peculiarity that one can randomly summon so many details of a person they've practically forgotten existed. Things between them were radically different following her panic attack that night. Sally became distant as if she purposely sought to avoid him. Every time he tried to call, her father would answer, always quickly changing the subject.

"Pastor James," he'd say, "does that mean she, uh, isn't home right now?"

"Yeah, no, she's here Benny, but what was I saying again? Ah yes,

God did this *really* wonderful thing for Job, you see, after Job's faith was tested..."

It would go on like that.

"But um, I just called to see if Sally can—"

"Wait, I didn't finish the *story*. You see, so then Judas threw the money back at the religious authorities and..."

He recalled that one day her father approached him. It was an awkward confrontation. Bennett was taking a piss when he walked into the church bathroom and stood at the urinal next to him. He felt Pastor James looking down at him, possibly even at his penis, though he couldn't be sure because he did not return glances.

"Benny, son."

Bennett zipped up his pants. "Uh, yeah?"

"I love your father as a brother in Christ but *please*, keep *that thing* away from *my* daughter. She's *not* going to date a Shepherd." He flushed, washed his hands, and left without saying a word more.

Later Bennett came to understand what he meant by "that thing" and "not going to date a Shepherd," his father a construction worker and not a successful *lawyer* or *banker* like many of the other congregants. He thought it ironic considering how Jesus is also said to have been a carpenter, a construction worker of sorts in his day. His parents continued attending church, giving away ten percent of their income each week until word broke out a few years later that Pastor James was a pervert. He was arrested and charged for molesting a handful of girls in the choir, including his own daughter. That was the first incident that caused Bennett to start questioning his Christian beliefs. If someone like his pastor, whom everyone adored, could be such a phony, why couldn't Jesus have been one too? Or his apostles? After all, everyone keeps skeletons in their closets and there has never been a shortage of frauds in the world.

He wondered how Sally was after all these years, contemplating the furtive abuse she endured under everyone's noses. Mya pawed his arm, hungry and eager to get him out of bed. "I spent the whole day sleeping," he said, yawning, looking at his phone. Two missed calls, one from the hospital and one from Eugene. He listened to the voicemails.

"You have seven saved messages and two new messages. First message."

"Hi," said a female voice, "I'm calling for Bennett Shepherd on behalf of Doctor Fischer. He would like to set an appointment with you as *soon* as possible. If you could call us back we can go over different options for treatment. *Please* give us a call at 555-473-9841. Thank you."

"Message saved. Second message."

"Hey dad, it's Gene. Sophie told me the news. I was thinkin' about'cha, hopin' I could get ahold of you. I'm tryin' to take leave so I can come home for a few weeks, spend the holidays stateside and see everyone. Anyway, call me back. Love ya."

He pressed re-dial.

"Hi, you've reached Eugene, I can't get to my phone right now but —"

[113]

He walked to his window and looked out at the evening sky. A few clouds hid the sun, still beaming as a gentle breeze kissed weak branches, toying with dying leaves. He grabbed his smokes and put his jacket on, settling upon his next course of action: a stroll up to Davis Park.

Hitting the sidewalk, the temperature cooler than the previous week, a Michigan winter slowly creeping in, his mind wandered back to Sally and his childhood years. They were cheerful for the most part. His parents were upstanding folks, unfailingly well-intentioned though oftentimes overprotective to the point of humiliation. He remembered the diamond where he and his siblings used to play baseball, his brother Jack a star player then, perhaps would have gone pro had he not gotten mixed up in the wrong crowd. Additionally, he thought about Teddy's, that old hamburger joint where his father took them as children, long since torn down.

He walked around the park lighting cigarette after cigarette, disregarding his condition, thinking about the "the good ol' days," missing Tomball. Growing up, he greatly admired Jack, an extraordinary athlete, the best baseball player on the Cougars of Tomball High School. It was Jack's senior year when he suffered a severe ankle sprain and got put on Percodan, the first turn down a slope that would later prove fatal. Towards the end Jack was heavy into coke and smack, the combination that did him in. February 27, 1979, Bennett still clearly recalled the moment he answered his phone, the horror of that night remaining with him like a detailed nightmare stamped into his brain. Losing Jack was one of the hardest things he'd ever gone through. His nerves *still* trembled whenever something triggered that memory.

He considered himself lucky for having survived all those years after Jack passed at twenty-seven. He was sixty-two now. A few hundred years ago he would have been among those deemed blessed. Even in modern times, how could he fret about dying when there were so many Jacks, so many juveniles who died victims of addiction and disease, poverty and war, never allowed the opportunity to live? Here he was, having lived a full life, the beneficiary of white, male, middle-class privilege in the United States, and he wanted to feel sorry for himself?

The death of his older brother, like the arrest of his former minister, was another pivotal step in his gradual departure from faith. It was the perceived betrayal by God and the ensuing emotional detachment he sensed that prompted him to seriously doubt everything he thought he knew about religion. He became an agnostic, retaining *aspects* of his faith that appeared meaningful: the Golden Rule, the story of Jesus, the lovelier tales and their elementary moral lessons. By the time his son Eugene was born, however, he was convinced that the good things in religion didn't rely on religion itself but instead rational principles; the bad things *were* religion—including the beliefs that humanity is inherently corrupt and deserving of punishment, that Jesus died a human sacrifice, that faith can save people's "souls." He found these doctrines absurd and profane. Years later, by happenstance, he learned

[115]

he wasn't the only unbeliever in his family; so was his cousin Jon in Virginia. Bennett walked through the park, recalling how that came about.

It was Christmas Eve, 1985. Jon, his parents, his three siblings, and the siblings' children traveled from Virginia to Texas as Bennett's father had offered to host them for the week. Along with the family, a few employees that worked for Bennett (this is when he had the minting business) were present at his father's as well. Having finished dinner, the kids horseplaying and shouting, the adults (mostly the women) in the kitchen cleaning or (mostly the men) in the living room watching television, Eugene—then a small boy—ran up to him.

"Daddy! I tink Gwandma is twapped in ta baffwomb."

"She's trapped in the bathroom?" Bennett went and knocked on the door. "Mom? You in there?" No answer. He tried to open it but it was locked. By this time his mother was already showing signs of mental illness, talking to herself, drinking more, smoking, which she had never done before. She even wandered off once and got lost downtown. When he finally busted open the door, to everyone's surprise the bathroom was empty. As a further matter, the window was open and her clothes were on the floor. She had gone wandering.

Everyone spent the next couple of hours frantically searching for her. Fortunately, unlike Detroit, the temperature in Tomball remains moderate during the winter so no one was worried about her getting sick or freezing to death. The police eventually located her walking aimlessly through the streets, dressed as if she had been readying to take a bath, wearing nothing but a towel. It was the first time his mother was hospitalized, where she remained for a week. Everyone gathered at the Shepherds that night to pray, believing they could invoke God's sympathy, have him intercede and do something though Bennett couldn't imagine what. During the prayers, he didn't close his eyes. He didn't buy into it a single bit. He knew they were talking to each other and vocalizing internal thoughts. That was all they were doing.

Looking around the room, everyone nodding their heads in agreement to the empty words, he noticed his cousin dozing on and off. Jon looked as disinterested as he did. Their eyes met and Bennett signaled that he wanted to step out for a smoke. They got up and excused themselves.

"I can't believe that shit tonight," Jon said, pulling out a match to kindle his cigarette.

"Yeah. Wait, you mean with *my mother* or that shit inside there?"

"Both."

"Yeah, it's ridiculous, a *prayer* intervention, give me a break. Please God," Bennett said, raising his hands, "I know you have a lot on your plate with wars, disease, poverty, and everything else in the world, but please, come rescue my mother's brain."

Jon smirked. "So I'm not the *only* one, eh?"

"Fuck no, I don't believe that shit. It's like *so many other* religions, Jon. You're a filthy human being who needs to be saved. Believe what I'm telling you and you'll be spared judgment. *Please*. Oldest trick in the book."

"Lucia know?"

"Nope. Nobody does... except you now. I'd prefer to keep it that way."

"I know what'cha mean."

Bennett's mind digressed from religion to his mother. It became obvious to the family after the incident on Christmas Eve that she was rapidly developing schizophrenia. Her health appeared to improve for a few months after she returned home until she was again caught acting irrational in public, on this occasion trying to rob a bank with a toy gun—something so profoundly uncharacteristic of his mother that everyone knew she was now a danger to herself. That's when she began spending time at the mental hospital, first days, then weeks. She would get released, seem to make improvement, and then end up back there. It was extremely difficult on the family, especially Bennett's father.

"I'm so embarrassed," he would say to Bennett. "Your mother is completely mad. All she does is talk about Jack Jr. like he's alive..."

The stress wore on the old man. Ultimately, on August 3, 1989, his mother drove another patient to the brink. "Have you seen Jack lately?" Bennett imagined her asking. "This is a picture of my Jack. He is going to be a pro-baseball player one day." The family was told that the other patient yanked a phone from the wall, tearing the handset from its chord, and struck her in the head with it repeatedly. She was sixty-seven years old. His father died of a heart attack two years later.

Bennett perched on a park bench, his mind all over the place. "What a life," he said, watching the sun slowly disappear as stars began to decorate the atmosphere. He thought about his life as a coin minter, how he acquired the business when he was twenty-one years old...

Back then it was a small enterprise owned by a man named Erwin, a neighbor who lived down the street from the Shepherds. All of the shop's electrical wiring and plumbing was installed by Bennett's father (aside from construction work, he was also especially handy) and the two men became close. Bennett took a keen interest in the minting process, always eager to accompany his father whenever Erwin needed something repaired or unclogged. Erwin eventually hired Bennett part-time to do odd jobs around the shop and get paid a little extra money under the table. He was a natural fit, passionate about the trade, learning how to mint coins and becoming one of the shop's best employees. When Erwin got older and fell ill, he decided to pass it on to Bennett as he had become like a son to him. After he died in 1977, Bennett took over ownership.

Manufacturing everything from custom coins for souvenir shops to trophies and plaques for various sporting events and businesses, he expanded the shop, doubling from four employees to eight and moving it to a larger space to house all their operations. Nevertheless, beginning in the '80s, Bennett's luck began to run dry. Profits didn't drop off at first. It was a steady decline until nearby rival company Planck Awards began dominating the market, scoring contracts with the U.S. military to produce medals and ribbons and then everything else in between—Public Safety awards to corporate commemorations. They swallowed the competition, including Bennett. By 1992, he was a boozer, bankrupt, his employees dwindling to a single person, and carrying on an affair with Angel.

As he sat alone in the park, lost in times past, the moon hovering overhead, a string of lamp posts producing an eerie but serene backdrop, his phone began ringing. "Eugene," it read on the screen.

"Hello? Gene?" he answered.

"Hey dad," Eugene said. "I'm glad I got ahold of you. How are ya?"

"Eh, I'm alright I guess. Hangin' in there. How've you been? I've missed you."

"I've missed you too, dad. I've been okay, keeping busy. I sent out a letter to ya last week, did ya get it?"

"No, I didn't get anything."

"It should be there soon. I sent you a picture of this big sea bass I caught, probably the biggest. You'll be impressed."

"I look forward to seeing it."

"So dad... Goodness, I don't know—how long—when did you find out about your heart? Sophie said they gave you months..."

"Yeah, found out last week. Collapsed at work..."

"Man... Were there any signs? I thought you were getting in shape?"

"Well, eh, ya know, I've had asthma for years, had a cough for some time too, shortness of breath here and there..."

"But you quit smokin'?"

Bennett didn't respond.

"Dad... And you don't have insurance?"

"Nope. Didn't have the extra cash to dole out. I've been savin' some up, needed it for retirement."

"Jesus, dad. You're *going to* quit smokin' at least, right?"

"I'm workin' on that."

"Well, I planned to come home next month for the holidays. I'm waiting for my request to get approved. I heard you might be going down to see the family."

"I'm strongly considering it."

"That'd be terrific. It's been what, twenty-five years since you've been down there?"

"Yeah, twenty-six. Long time."

"I think it'd be good for you and Sophie. She's still *pretty* upset."

"Yeah, we talked for a good two hours on the phone the other morning, on Saturday I think it was."

"She told me about it. I know she's still unsure whether she wants to see you or not but I think she'll come around. I told her she should."

"Really? I got the impression that she wanted to see me..."

"Yeah, sure dad, I mean she does but it's still difficult for her. She thinks it's unfair that you've ignored her all these years and now suddenly want to re-enter her life, when you're ill and all. She thinks you're going to abandon her again."

[121]

He began to feel tears well up in his eyes. "Ignore her? *Abandon* her? Those were *never* my intentions..."

"I know but that's how she sees it. I'm not sayin' she's right."

"How—how do *you* see it?"

"You know, we've talked about it over the years. It *was* tough on us when you left. It hurt. I was angry at you for a long time but we've worked through it I think. I'm grown now, I understand what you did."

"You do?"

"Yeah, dad. Raising a family is *hard*. I'm sure I must've been a pain in the ass," he said with a chuckle. "Why do you think *I* never had kids?"

Bennett laughed a little too.

The two talked until Eugene had to go. He said he'd be in touch, gave Bennett the standard line that he'd keep him in his thoughts and prayers. Bennett hung up and continued walking through the dimly lit park, staring at the vast empty space above, imagining innumerable worlds that must also be suffering, neglected by any supreme creator. *What's all this for?* Contemplating his son and daughter, he suddenly felt sadness overpower him. He fell to the grass and wept, speaking as if his daughter stood before him.

"I'm sorry," he sobbed, "*I'm so sorry.* I'm not ready to die yet... not yet..."

Sometimes he wished he was religious and this was one of those moments. He knew he couldn't simply force himself to believe something because he *wanted* it to be true or because it made him *feel* better. He generally didn't desire to believe that any of mankind's gods could be real and he was confident in his many reasons for rejecting them. Other times, however, he understood the allure of thinking that a heavenly father looked down from above, loving and caring for all of his children, each uniquely created and bestowed with cosmic significance, the Earth nothing but a sort of exam for one particular species of primate. For better or worse, Bennett simply couldn't convince himself that this fantastic tale in any way mirrored the Universe he lived in. Death wasn't the beginning of an eternal, blithe existence somewhere in another dimension; it was the end of a brief, arduous one on a queer, humble planet that some creatures came to call Earth. He knew this to be true in his heart, as well as his intellect, even though his heart longed for more.

Part II

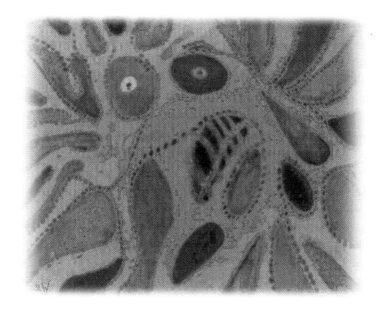

X.

Only dreams

The next two weeks were largely uneventful. Bennett spent most hours in his apartment sulking, reminiscing over his life, noting each passing day as he edged nearer to his ultimate demise. The letter from his son arrived in the mail after they spoke on the phone, along with a photograph of an enormous bass he caught in the Yellow Sea. Bennett admired the photo and added it to the collection in his closet. The passive monotony of the days were briefly interrupted by calls from Dave and Fred and a few spontaneous visits from Sara here and there. After quitting the steel mill, Bennett was forced to tell his co-workers the truth about his condition as they came to suspect a change in his air and persisted in phoning him until he confessed. Their reaction to the news was predictable: shocked silence, sympathy, utter helplessness. Of course, Bennett tried to play it down, thanked them for their support, and said he'd be in touch. His only real human connection during this period was his neighbor, who on one afternoon brought him a plate of chocolate chip cookies.

"So... Leon asked me out on a date tonight!" Sara exclaimed. It was the happiest Bennett had seen her. She wore a blazing smile, bursting with life as if a switch inside had suddenly flickered on. He appreciated that, along with the cookies. Her radiance contagious, it relieved his sobriety, if only for the short duration of her stay. She also came over a couple of times to see Mya.

"I wonder what she is trying to say to us when she meows."

"Why don't you ask her? But she only understands Spanish! Barriga llena, corazón contento!"

"I didn't know you spoke Spanish."

"My sister sees a guy—he's practically my brother-in-law—it's his first language. I've picked up a few words from her over the years."

"What's it mean?"

"'A full belly and a happy heart!'"

Sometimes she failed to understand his sense of humor, though he wasn't *that* funny to begin with. Beyond fleeting visits he didn't see too much of her during the final two weeks of October. He kept busy to himself and almost everyday she worked and went to school. Much of his time was spent on the phone with secretaries from the hospital advising him to come back in to see the good doctor.

"Mr. Shepherd, I know this is very difficult for you," they would say, "but you *need* to see Doctor Fischer. Have you thought about hospice care?"

"You know what? Go fuck yourself!"

That's how those conversations typically went. He was also in regular contact with different churches that ran charities for the poor, the sick, the hungry, etc. He was told they would help in any way possible but it was clear he wouldn't get a transplant. The most they could do was assist in paying for medications and treatments, which

[127]

could prolong his life briefly, perhaps lessen the anxiety and pain of the experience. It would not cure his heart disease. Death was still in the cards even though he *might* be able to buy himself a few more months. And if he were to receive assistance, the ten grand he had in the bank would be purged from his account. Charities aren't interested in pooling together funds to help people with ten grand on hand when there are those, sick or homeless, who literally have nothing but their namesake. He understood and decided to simply continue the medications he was on, not wishing to spend his last days in hospitals and doctors' offices. In a couple of weeks, he reminded himself, I'll go to Virginia and then to Texas. That was his only plan.

When he wasn't being unproductive, wasting away in front of the television, he spent a great deal of time reading, writing, and going on walks. In two weeks he finished *The Selfish Gene,* then went on to start and complete *Staring At The Sun* by Irvin Yalom and *The Portable Nietzsche,* translated by Walter Kaufmann, both of which he picked up at a local bookstore during one of his afternoon ambles. They offered invaluable insights, helping to put irrepressible emotions into their proper contexts, and inspired him to attempt a draft of the book he'd always wanted to write. The result was the same each time: get a few pages in, then scrap it or lose interest. He grew discouraged until Sara suggested he write down the dreams he was continuing to experience.

"You know, perhaps if you write them down," she said, combing Mya's fur, "it can help form the basis of that book you're struggling to write."

"Are you tryin' some psychoanalysis bullshit on me?"

And so he started recording every dream he had. Each morning, he'd wake up, stretch his arms, and go straight to his café table. Mya would meow desperately to get him to feed her breakfast...

"Hold on, Mya," he said, sitting down to collect his thoughts. He looked at the time and date on his phone.

"9:23 A.M., October 30, 2018" he wrote on the top right hand corner of the page. He noted that it was 'Devil's Night.'

"I saw myself dead last night," he wrote. "I was in a funeral home, everyone around me crying, reminiscing over my dad. The poster board in the chapel read 'Jack Shepherd Sr.' It highlighted his talents as a handyman, the overall hard worker he was. There were different pictures of him doing construction, plumbing, mowing the grass with a very young Jack Jr., other pictures of him with my mother, the family, Erwin. I felt disoriented because a lot of people who didn't know my dad were there—old friends, past girlfriends—and everyone seemed to be ignoring me.

"I went up to the casket to pay my respects. The first thing I noticed was the dusty brown suit jacket on the corpse. It was Erwin's old jacket. I think I still have that stored away somewhere. Then my eyes traveled upwards to the cosmetic face. It was myself lying in the coffin, nearly unrecognizable beneath the thick layers of makeup. I looked content, tranquil, well-prepared to become worm food. I began overhearing conversations people were having with one another.

'It's too bad he never knew Jesus.'

'Deep down he was still a believer.'

'He seemed bitter.'

"I wanted to laugh. As I turned back to make my way through the crowd of mourners, I started shoving people, perhaps to see whether or not they were illusions? To test my authority? I don't know. It's what I did in the dream. They ended up kicking me out of the funeral home, said I was ruining my father's dignity, that I needed to ask God for forgiveness. This part of the dream approximately corresponds to actual events. I also want to note for anyone who may read this in the future that I do not want a religious service when I die.

"The next thing I remember is wandering the streets with a bottle of whiskey in my hand. I drank but it never ran out, not a single drop. I stumbled along as if intoxicated, dirty and ruffled though I was in a suit and tie. I also noticed that movement required much effort, as if heavy weights were tied to my ankles. I came to the MacArthur Bridge. It appeared to be early morning and a dense fog made it virtually impossible to see anything beyond twenty feet or so. I climbed over the railing and stepped right up to the edge, staring down at the filthy waters below. This part of the dream also approximately corresponds to actual events.

"I woke up a moment ago with this question looping in my mind. It was 'Whose God? *Who's* God?' It made me think about my dad for some reason. I could almost hear him ask in his very matter-of-fact tone: 'Who are we to question God?'"

[130]

Bennett put his pen down and lit a cigarette. Who are we not to question man's gods? He reflected on a conversation he and Sam had over the phone many months back.

"You're very blessed, ya know," Sam said.

"Nah, just lucky."

"There's no such thing as luck, bro."

"Of course there is. That's *all* there is. Somebody's gotta win the game and somebody's gotta lose it."

"And what *is* the game?"

"Chance and necessity."

Bennett opened up the window and gazed out, blowing cigarette smoke into the air, still not completely awake. Across the parking lot he spotted a sparrow perched on a telephone wire, chirping by its lonesome. He regarded it with affection, sat back down at his table, and tried to analyze the meaning of his dreams, those stockpiled time capsules hidden in the innermost retreats of his brain. He recalled fragments of his past, his father's funeral twenty-seven years back. He *was* kicked out for objecting to the minister's eulogy, to the worship songs. I stood up for common sense, he reminisced. I told everyone right then and there that they were lying to themselves, that dad wasn't in heaven. I told them they were wasting their lives, that there were real problems in the world, that they wouldn't solve them by talking to an invisible superman in the sky. He couldn't help but reflect on his former zeal with a dash of embarrassment. What did it really matter in the end?

Outside he noticed that the sparrow had multiplied from one to a few dozen, stretched across the wire, shoulder to shoulder, wing to wing, chirping, singing, whatever it is groups of them do. Maybe they're spreading the latest gossip or exchanging secrets about where to find the tastiest seeds? Or, more likely, evoking what he'd ascertained from *The Selfish Gene*, they were engaging in some form of manipulation.

He flipped back a few pages in his notebook and read some of his logs from recent days. According to one, dated "5:23 A.M., October 22," he dreamt he was trapped in a bubble, drifting through space...

"Though it made no sense, I felt sublime, peaceful, overjoyed. At first I assumed I was ascending into heaven, certain that I must have died. Unfortunately, I quickly realized this couldn't be the case as others were coasting along in bubbles too, including Sam, Marty, my cousin, and my old foreman. I knew this could only be a dream rather than paradise because if God were truly good then no way in hell would John be there."

He'd also written that he saw Jesus in his dream, the white European one popularized in Western culture: blue eyes, a brown beard, wearing a white robe. Jesus was also inside a protective bubble randomly drifting through space, the expression on his face obscured. Bennett might have been more intrigued had he not learned to expect the inane during sleep. Bennett's bubble moved through the aether until it came to rest in a lavish field of green, acutely resembling Davis Park, the one he frequently walked to. He noted it strange that as he descended, there was nothing but the dark Universe surrounding him, galaxies and shooting stars in the distance, yet when he came upon the field and looked up, outer space was replaced by blue skies, assemblies of massive puffy clouds, flocks of birds, and a bright fiery sun.

"I noticed Jasmine sitting in the field, in a circular mound of dirt, candles all around her, chanting in a language I couldn't understand. I surmised that she was casting some type of Wiccan spell in hopes of curing me of this illness. I fell onto my back and could not get up. Someone approached me but it was not Jasmine... It was Angel. She walked over to me and began touching my face. My bubble had vanished. She undressed me... when I awoke I had difficulty breathing... Chest felt like a pile of bricks lay upon it," his log ended.

Again he looked up from his notebook and watched the sparrows. More flocked to the wire while others flew away, their song never ceasing as though it had no end. He scrolled to another page, dated "2:17 A.M., October 26." It took place in Houston, at the mall off Tomball Parkway. He was with Lucia and the kids. It appeared to be the spring of '91 "because Sophia was pleading with us to buy her damn near everything we passed for her upcoming sixth birthday. The mall was relatively busy as it had been in real life. We were walking along and out of nowhere I spotted Angel casually looking at a display of sunglasses. Angel and I were dating a month or so at that point; that was a few weeks after my dad passed away. I froze."

[133]

He wasn't sure if what he'd written more accurately represented the dream from a few nights before or the memory that it pertained to.

"I approached, begging her to stop following me," he continued reading. "At that moment Lucia and the children walked over."

He could still call to mind the words Lucia spoke to him that day in the mall. It felt so long ago and yet here it remained in the back of his head, clear as crystal, unbeknownst until today.

"*This* is the one who told you to close the shop and liquidize the assets? Bennett, she looks like she's *barely* out of college. *This* is the girl that Simeon recommended?"

Angel *had* been his financial adviser recommended by a family friend at church, he mused, appreciating the incongruity. She really did convince me to close the minting business, divorce my wife, leave Texas to work for her father in Detroit. What it must have felt like for Lucia. He did still feel a little guilty after all these years. It wasn't until six months after the run-in with Angel at the mall that his wife discovered their affair via a hotel thank-you-postcard sent through the mail.

His log continued:

"I don't remember what happened next but as the dream continued, terror struck me and I fell to the ground, clutching my chest. Everyone gathered around me. Dave, Fred, John, everyone from work was there, huddling over my body, trying to help me regain myself. 'Call 911!' someone yelled. That's when I woke up a few minutes ago. Once again my breathing felt strained. I coughed a bit, drank a glass of water, feeling better."

[134]

He deliberated about his heart attack at work weeks earlier, the panic he experienced, the faces of his children all he could visualize in that instant. How much he missed them! He sighed as nostalgia plucked on his entrails like a somber violinist, closing the notebook, returning a glance out the window. The sparrows were gone. The telephone wire hung in silence, absent of their melody. Everything is transient, he thought. After I'm gone, the world will continue on as before, the future as mysterious and unpredictable as ever in solidarity with an all but forgotten past. He continued staring off into space, meditating on that idea until both his and Mya's stomachs were growling. He fed her and opened the refrigerator to see what he could make for himself.

"We're lookin' pretty empty, Mya."

He made a grocery list and took a shower, his mind still captivated by the meaning of his most recent dream.

Does it have a meaning? he pondered, scrubbing his arms under the hot water. Do any of them? He questioned himself as he stepped out and got dressed. Whatever emerged from his subconscious during the night, it left him feeling more optimistic than the days and weeks prior. It was like a burden had been lifted off his shoulders. He searched around in his closet and located the dusty brown suit jacket that Erwin had given him decades previously. It was a tighter fit than he remembered but he wore it anyway. He left his apartment, whistling the theme song from The Pink Panther, his favorite film as a boy. When

[135]

he got to the bottom of his staircase he spotted Sara entering Willow Lane.

"Hey neighbor!" he called out as she approached.

"Oh, hey Bennett," she said cheerfully. "I haven't seen you around much the last few days. Doin' alright? Nice jacket by the way."

"Thanks. Yeah, I'm doin' well. Where's your boyfriend? No Leon today?"

"Nah, had a dentist appointment this morning, gotta work later this afternoon. But he's comin' over tomorrow."

"Things workin' out for you guys, eh?"

"Uh huh. Hey, I meant to ask you, do you have any plans tomorrow night for Halloween? Leon and I were thinkin' about cookin' up steaks. Might make pumpkin pie too. Wanna come?"

He hesitated. "It sounds wonderful but I don't wanna intrude on your romantic dinner or anything."

"Please! I'd love to have you over. I've been meaning to catch up with you, see how you've been holdin' up."

"Well, if you insist, I guess I could come by. What'cha doin' right now?"

"Nothin'. Just gettin' home, was gonna hang out 'til work. You?"

"Well, I was goin' up to the grocery store... Wanna grab a coffee?"

"Sure!"

The two got into Bennett's car, navigating side streets until they arrived at a parking lot.

"Telly's?" she said as they pulled in. "I haven't been here since I was kid. I didn't even realize this place was still here."

"It's kinda hidden. I used to come up here a lot, brought my son a few times when he was in town visiting too."

They found a booth and ordered coffee.

"Have you figured shit out with, uh, your living arrangements?" he asked after they had scanned the menus. "Whether you're going to stay in school and move back home with your mom or..."

"Not quite. I have until the end of the year to figure it out, that's when my lease is up. Leon says he has some friends who are looking for roommates. We might able to move in with—"

"Whoa, whoa," he interrupted. "*We?* You and Leon are talking about movin' in *together?* You guys have been seein' each other for what, like *two* weeks? *At most?*"

She rolled her eyes. "Look, he knows my situation is desperate, he's tryin' to be supportive. Christ, I dunno where I'd be without him! He's been a godsend these last couple of weeks."

"I know where you'd be, Sara. You'd be where you are now. Your strength in overcoming is yours and yours alone. You simply can't imagine you're capable of it because you don't believe in yourself."

"Well, well," she grinned, sipping her coffee. "Aren't you suddenly *the* optimist. Where the hell did *you* come from?"

"Remember a couple of weeks ago, when you stopped by with that roast you made, which was goddamn *amazing* by the way, and you told me to write down my dreams?"

"Yeah, you start doin' that?"

"Mm-hmm. Well, the one I had last night...."

"What was it about?"

"Random shit mostly. I was at my dad's funeral, or my funeral, I dunno, caused a big scene, got kicked out."

"Oh my god! Did something like that happen? At your—your dad's—"

"Somethin' like that, yeah. Anyway, then I found myself on the MacArthur bridge, the one in Detroit that goes to Belle Isle."

"What were ya doin' there?"

"I think I was contemplating suicide."

"Jesus. In—in your dream?"

"Sort of... Well no, that happened in real life, years ago. I was forty-one, at the top of my game really, had money, everything I could ever want, but I was completely miserable inside. I was a wreck then."

"Why?" she asked, dumbfounded.

"At the time, I hated life, working as a mortgage consultant, separated from my children. I was either gonna go insane doin' what I was doin' or quit and figure out what I wanted with my life."

"And so you quit and figured it out?"

He laughed. "Figured it out? No. *But* I sure as hell figured out what I *didn't* want!"

"So... What's that gotta do with *anything*?"

"Well, my point is that no matter what happens, no matter how depressed you get, how lost you feel, don't give up. And don't rely on others for your happiness or security. All you have in the darkest hours is yourself. I think that might've been what I was working out in my dream... Because those hours, those moments, they're only temporary. They're fleeting. Pain is as fleeting as joy. All you have is now."

"Bennett, you're preaching to the choir. That's always been my philosophy. But the 'now' we're always enslaved to can get pretty shitty at times... It's not like I have to convince you of that. Besides, I *really like* Leon. I'm not just using him for support."

"Yeah, I'm sorry. It's not my place. You talk to Tom anymore?"

She glared at him.

"Oh, is that bad? What?" He hadn't realized he wasn't supposed to mention that name again.

"We're not *talking* about Tom... I'll be right back." She got out of the booth. "I have to use the ladies' room. If the waitress returns, can you tell her I'd like a half order of French toast?"

"Sure."

He sat looking around the diner, bustling with idle chatter, one TV on the wall in the corner showing a steady stream of headlines. Does anyone actually read all that scrolling text? *What am I doing here?* At that instant his ears perked up to a conversation nearby.

"What about that guy you called, that one on the radio?" a woman asked.

"Donaldson?" another woman responded. "God, what a con-artist he was. Worst decision I ever made."

"What happened again?"

"Pete died and I still had a ridiculous amount of debt from the

[139]

operations. That guy didn't help us at all."

Bennett smiled, thinking about his drive home from Anchor Bay a couple of weeks earlier. "Guess I dodged a bullet."

The waitress came by and he put in the request, a half order of French toast for Sara and a Western omelet for him.

"Hey, have you figured out when you're leaving Michigan?" she questioned upon returning to her seat.

"Yeah, leaving on the thirteenth of next month."

"In like two weeks? And that's it? You're not comin' back?" she asked, dejected.

"Aw, c'mon now, you can never say never. If I can have it my way, I'll go down there, maybe spend a month or two, and then come home. We'll have to see how things go."

"Have you spoken with your daughter any more? Worked things out? Last time you told me she was having second thoughts about everything."

"Yeah, yeah, we talked some more, she's gonna try and put up with me, give it her best shot. That's all I can ask for."

When they finished eating, Bennett paid the tab and drove her back to the apartments.

"Bennett," she said upon exiting his car, "the dreams we have, what if *that's* actual reality?"

"What'cha mean?"

"Like they're a window into a world beyond this one... All

[140]

possibilities existing together in some other dimension only perceptible in dreams. No time, no space, nothing but a stream of pure consciousness."

"Consciousness, of course, but I dunno about that other stuff. Dreams are pretty consistent with prior waking states."

"Well, thanks for shooting that idea down!"

"But I guess I'll find out soon enough."

"You talk about death so callously. Aren't you scared?"

"Absolutely. The prospect that my body — *my* flesh — will turn cold, stiff, rot away beneath the dirt, that's especially unnerving. But I've also always known this life is temporary, for everyone and everything in it, from stars to microbes to people. If I go to sleep and wake up, I expect I'll be pleasantly surprised. If I don't, and being dead *is* nothing at all, I have *nothing* to worry about. I've accepted that possibility, that the latter is probably true. The only rational response to it is the one Epicurus formulated: 'Where I am, death is not. Where death is, I am not.' So why let it bother me so much? Who knows though, maybe I'll realize all of my experiences on earth were only a fraction of reality."

"Like all *this*, all of the things we perceive," she said, extending her arms, "they're only illusions, like Plato's shadow people?"

"Sure," he said, scratching his chin. "Or like you said, in some way or another, only dreams."

XI.

Black hole

Bennett pushed his cart through the grocery store, checking items off his list, enjoying a serenity he hadn't experienced in weeks. He observed the selection of delicious fruits and vegetables, picking them up, smelling them, appreciating their color, texture, scent. Walking up to the registers, he resolved he should buy a pumpkin, figuring if this was in fact his last Halloween he wouldn't spend it moping around. He wanted to live, soaking up every opportunity and reveling in the mundane pleasures of human existence while his heart still beat. He picked the largest, roundest, orangest pumpkin he could find and went to stand in line, contemplating what he would carve into it.

"Bennett!" a voice called as he loaded his groceries onto the conveyer belt.

He turned around. Marty from Tuesday night poker waved from the next line over. Marty was tall and skinny with short blonde hair and glasses, in his early fifties, still a loan originator though at a different firm than the one he and Bennett had worked at years earlier.

"Hey Marty!" he said over the other shoppers. "How're ya doin'?"

"Good! For Chrissakes, I wasn't sure if you were alive! Don't you answer your phone anymore?"

After Bennett finished paying for his groceries, he pushed his cart to the exit where Marty stood waiting.

"Sorry," he said, shaking Marty's hand. "I didn't wanna shout over everybody."

"What the fuck, Bennett? You haven't been at poker for three weeks now, haven't returned my calls. All the fellas been wonderin' what happened to you. What's wrong, you tryin' to avoid us?"

"Nah, Marty, been busy with work and stuff, ya—"

"Bullshit," he cut in. "I ran into that little Iranian chic you used to date, over at The Showcase."

"Oh?"

"She told me everything. Told me you're..."

"Goddamn it, Jazz," Bennett muttered. "I didn't want everyone to find out like that."

"When were you gonna say somethin'? She said you plan on leavin' town soon?"

"In a couple of weeks. I was gonna let you guys know, Marty. I just haven't been ready."

"Well, shit! We gotta celebrate your last days here! We're gonna throw a goin' away party for you!"

"What? No," Bennett objected. "Who is?"

"Me, the guys, it'll be great. Invite anyone you want. When do you leave?"

"November thirteenth, uh, it's a Tuesday, I believe."

"Alright! We'll throw the party the night before, on Monday! Or would Sunday work better?"

[143]

"Marty, hold up, I really don't—"

"Oh shut up, Bennett! You avoided me all this time, now I'm tryin' to do ya a favor and ya throw a hissy fit? Christ, what a guy you are!"

"I appreciate it, I do, but—"

"No buts. Monday, the twelfth, mark it on your calendar. I'll get shit set up, you worry about who you want to invite! I gotta go but I'll call you later! Answer this time!"

Bennett drove home, murmuring to himself that he did not want a going away party. What is this, he wondered, a celebration of my death? On second thought, the idea didn't seem totally absurd. He pulled into Willow Lane, unloaded his groceries and prepared what he'd coined his "World Famous Bennett Shepherd's Pie." Obviously, it wasn't world famous but his version was scrumptious nonetheless.

For the filling:

    1 tablespoon of olive oil

    1 tablespoon of butter

    1 large diced onion

    2 chopped stalks of celery

    1 can of corn

    2 pounds of lean ground lamb

    3 cloves of minced garlic

    1/2 cup of flour

    1 teaspoon of paprika

    1 tablespoon of ketchup

1/8 teaspoon of cinnamon

1/2 teaspoon of minced fresh rosemary

A dash of garlic salt

Salt and pepper to taste

For the mashed potato topping he mixed:

5 large peeled and mashed Russet potatoes

1 1/2 cups of grated white cheddar cheese

2 tablespoons of butter

1/2 cup of cream cheese

1 egg yolk beaten with 2 tablespoon of 2% milk

A pinch of cayenne

Mya purred as it cooked in the oven, the mouthwatering scent appeasing her and Bennett both. He made enough for himself and some to take to Sara's the following day.

He sat down in his recliner, plate in hand, flipping through television channels, failing to find much. Ping Pawn was on but he wasn't in the mood for it. To his satisfaction, he managed to locate a science program about black holes. It reminded him of drifting through space in his dream.

"Stellar black holes," the narrator said, "are the final evolutionary stage in the lifetimes of stars so massive, they were once twenty-five times heavier than our Sun. To put that in perspective, the weight of the Sun, written in kilograms, is two followed by thirty zeroes."

Bennett contemplated that until his head felt woozy. "Hey, maybe I'll become a black hole," he said to Mya.

The narrator continued, informing him that the Milky Way galaxy alone contains some 200 billion stars and millions upon millions of black holes, that the *observable* Universe was estimated to be 93 billion light-years in diameter. Knowing that light travels at approximately 186,000 miles *per second*, he pulled up the calculator on his phone, continuing his commentary to the cat.

"There are 86,400 seconds in a day, which means..." He put in some more numbers. Mya pawed at one of her toys inattentively as he explained. "There are 31 million, 536 thousand seconds in a 365-day year, which means in one year light travels roughly 5.8 trillion miles. And the observable Universe, in mileage, is 93 billion *times that*."

Now his head was really spinning, those numbers far too large for him to compute on his phone calculator. "And people believe that *all* of this exists for *them*."

After the program concluded he switched over to the local news broadcast.

"Officials are asking Detroit residents to keep an eye out in their communities for Angel's Night tonight," the newswoman said, "and thousands have already volunteered to help prevent arson. Over to you, Bill."

"Hi Sabrina. I interviewed dozens of volunteers earlier today about their efforts to patrol their neighborhoods and here's what some of them had to say."

"This ain't Devil's Night anymore," declared a volunteer. "This is Angel's Night and we hope people's better angels will prevail

[146]

because..."

Bennett turned off the TV, yawning and lighting a cigarette. "I better carve this pumpkin before it's too late," he told Mya, who slept on the couch. He walked into the kitchen and pulled out a butcher's knife, studying the pumpkin and thinking about what he wanted to carve. He glanced over at Mya, still snoring.

"I know," he said, noticing Mya's orange fur and the pumpkin shared a similar hue. He got to work, first removing the top, then cutting, carving, and slicing the eyes, ears, nose, mouth, and whiskers. After he finished nearly two hours later, he set the pumpkin on a small end table near the window and stepped back to admire his accomplishment. He had done well for an amateur. It looked distinguishably feline, probably the best pumpkin he'd ever carved. He picked Mya up, carried her off to bed, and fell asleep.

The following morning he awoke and immediately went to his café table, lighting a cigarette and pulling out his notebook, his dream log. "October 31, 2018," he jotted. "Slept like a black hole, a very deep sleep. Had a dream that I was carving a pumpkin with Lucia and the kids at our home in Texas. The kids were very young, Gene maybe only seven. I cut my hand and ran to the sink to wash it out. Lucia started asking me whose blood it was, became very angry. Then I woke up."

He shook his head, unable to decipher the significance of the dream or why old memories frequently resurfaced, remarkably precise in some aspects but failing to parallel reality in others.

[147]

For an unknown reason, an urge came over him to drive to the dog park near Lake St. Clair, the one he used to take his Greyhound to. Even after Shiva died he'd go there once in a while, finding something peaceful about watching the other dogs and their owners, feeling a kinship to them. He never got another dog, however. Many of the places he subsequently lived, such as Willow Lane, didn't allow them.

He fed Mya, showered and left, grabbing his coat and a tattered Bible, The King James Version. For another inexplicable reason, he desired to read his favorite book of the Bible, the only one he could occasionally relate to, the book of Ecclesiastes.

There weren't many people at the dog park when he arrived. It was a chilly day, temperature in the high 40's, the sun battling clouds for visibility. He sat down on a bench with his Bible in hand and watched the dogs, a Labrador, a Bullmastiff mix, two Pugs, and a Beagle. The Labrador and Bullmastiff picked on the Beagle, which in turn harassed the two Pugs, themselves trying to attack each other, oblivious to everyone else. Watching them brought a cheer to his demeanor. He opened his Bible to Ecclesiastes and began reading. Beautiful poetry but this author sounds beyond depressed, he noted, coming across passages like the following:

"If a man beget an hundred children, and live many years, so that the days of his years be many, and his soul be not filled with good, and also that he have no burial; I say, that an untimely birth is better than he. For he cometh in with vanity, and departeth in darkness, and his name shall be covered with darkness.

Moreover he hath not seen the sun, nor known any thing: this hath more rest than the other. Yea, though he live a thousand years twice told, yet hath he seen no good: do not all go to one place?"

In other words, for those who fail to find the goodness in life, it might be more optimal to have never been born. And yet, he thought, even the very idea of goodness as a conceptual experience derived from this world appears to some inadequate. As the second verse in the book declares:

"Vanity of vanities, saith the Preacher, vanity of vanities; all is vanity."

This theme throughout the work always made Bennett feel slightly better about his trivial concerns, made him think that perhaps being dead wouldn't amount to missing out on too much after all. Have I found the goodness in life? he asked himself. He peered around, a sense of harmony swelling his insides. The irony that he sat here in a dog park, without a dog of his own, an atheist in the clenches of death, reading the Bible, wasn't lost on him. If the Preacher of Ecclesiastes lamented the absurdity of life, he couldn't help but laugh.

As he convened there and read, a man with a Golden Retriever approached and sat down on the bench next to him. He was an older gentleman, clean cut, wearing glasses, possessing a grandfatherly quality even to Bennett. Bennett tried to conceal the book in his hand, wishing to avoid the impression that he belonged to the faithful or was interested in theological drivel.

"What'cha reading?" the man asked, leaning over.

[149]

"Oh, uh—it's uh," Bennett stammered, "the book of Ecclesiastes."

"Hmm. That's quite a pessimistic work, painful to read sometimes."

"Yeah," Bennett agreed. "Eloquently paints a meaningless picture, I've heard it described."

The man chuckled. "For the unbeliever, yes, life is meaningless."

Bennett's internal voice snickered: Oh, so that's what kind of fellow you are.

"But," he responded, "do you really think somethin' like God or Thor or Poseidon can create meaning in a way that real-life experiences cannot?"

Assessing Bennett, the man thought to himself: Oh, so that's what kind of fellow you are.

"Thor, Poseidon, no," he answered, "but Jesus Christ, yes. He is the reason I get up everyday. He's the reason I've spent the last fifty years in ministry, sitting on the bedside of the sick, telling them with a straight face that they can remain hopeful, that their lives weren't meaningless, that Jesus is waiting for them on the other side. That's what makes Jesus' crucifixion such a powerful act, an example of how we too can willingly embrace our cross when the time comes to bear it."

"That's an interesting way to interpret it. You're a minister?"

"At Hope Lutheran, right there." He pointed down the street at a snow-white building with a tall steeple. "Jerome."

"Bennett."

The men shook hands.

"But how is that genuine?" Bennett carried on. "How does positing

[150]

Jesus as your reason for living or dying accomplish anything meaningful that children or your career or your country or life itself cannot? Those things are tangible, their effects actually matter."

"Because," Jerome replied, "Jesus lasts forever and does not change. Children grow old, move away, pass on. Careers fail, leave us unfulfilled. Nothing in life is stable but Jesus is. He's the same yesterday, today, and tomorrow..."

"Why Jesus though? Why not the Flying Spaghetti Mon—"

"Did the Flying Spaghetti Monster die for you?"

Bennett grinned, aware that their worldviews were so distant from one another, like two foreign languages, communication all but useless.

"I don't see the world like that," Bennett said. "I don't see humanity as inherently evil or in need of a savior, especially one in the superficial sense of blood offering. Sure, we're brutes, savages, we kill and steal like every other animal. The central point of atonement through the sacrifice of an innocent creature glorifies that savagery. But *it's our humanity that allows us to redeem ourselves.* We've evolved the capacity to reason, to establish morals, to turn against our genes, against the natural order of things. I do find life fulfilling. Coming here, speaking with you, that's fulfilling in some way I suppose. In my view, being human is our greatest asset. It sounds like in your religion being human is our damnation."

"I guess I don't have that much faith in human beings," Jerome laughed.

"Me neither. But whatever faith I do possess, it's in myself and the

[151]

physical laws that keep everything in motion. I'm only responsible for my actions, my happiness, my reaction to the joys and sufferings in the world. What concern is your God to me or I to him?"

"The apostle Paul said, 'I do not understand my own actions. For I do not do what I want, but I do the very thing I hate.' How can you, as an unbeliever, take responsibility for anything when you're nothing more than a product of your genes, your environment, a coalescence of matter and energy reacting to an unintelligent, determined process guided by nothing but natural laws?"

The Golden Retriever ran up to them and laid down in the grass next to the bench.

"The same way St. Paul did, also bound by those same natural laws that essentially determine who each person turns out to be. We call the result a will."

"Ah, but I *believe* in free will," Jerome said. "Without God, there is no free will, no purpose. Your decision to do good rather than evil is no more your free choice than it was your choice to possess the genes you do."

"I don't think so," Bennett said. "I won't pretend to understand how free will works any more than you do— *no one* fully understands consciousness and the role it plays—but whatever it is, or if it is, I can still observe that I *seem* freer than say, your Golden Retriever. I'm able to gauge my options, weigh the various potential outcomes my actions might bring. Even if free will is nothing more than an illusion, it's a practical one, powerful enough too. From that we establish ideas and norms for how to improve our lives or those around us, ya know, rather than destroy each other and the world."

"That's very noble but why should I feel the same? What if I'm one of the many sociopaths in society whose interests lie solely in myself? Who are you to tell me I'm wrong?"

"Who am I *not* to tell you you're wrong? Of course, my opinion isn't *by virtue* special or better than yours but you may discern it to be *more or less informed*. The same can be said about your religion versus say, the Mormon religion. That's why nothing is more important than rational, honest, *open* dialogue. If I can reason enough people to my side and we decide you're a danger to society, then we lock you up. Our ability to apprehend the causes that *underlie* our experiences, using all the tools at our disposal, is *key* to solving our problems. Like I said, *that's* where true redemption lies."

"Ah, so might is right!"

"If that's what you decide. I can't *prove* you wrong but I don't have to agree or follow your moral philosophy. In the end, what one perceives as valuable is subjective in *some* sense."

"And what about when you die?" Jerome asked. "What happens then? You're simply dead, that's it? What assurances lie in that?"

"Does the Universe owe us assurances?"

"But how could anyone have hope in this life if they know they're going to die and everything they've experienced is consequently snuffed out from existence? Their conscious reality, any sense of achievement, annihilated!"

[153]

"Life is bigger than any one person. Sure, we won't always be around to witness the impact of our actions... but others may come along and build upon them."

"Until the Universe burns up!"

"But so what? What matters is 'now,' right? I forget where I heard it said but the past is nothing more than presently experienced memories and the future is nothing more than presently experienced anticipation."

"That's one way of looking at it."

"What else could matter?"

"Tomorrow? Next month? Next year?"

"Well sure," Bennett said with a smile. "By all means plan ahead but do so for *this reality*, not one confined only to the imagination. What good is next month on earth when we'll be enjoying ourselves in eternity anyway?"

He proceeded to tell Jerome about his heart disease, how his feelings about it didn't compute, how *death* didn't make much sense.

"Death is like a black hole," Bennett said, "there doesn't seem to be any logic to it, nothing that appeals to our instincts."

Jade, the Golden Retriever, napped by her master's feet, bored and tired from playing with the other dogs. Jerome, believing it was his duty, attempted to share the Gospel with Bennett but he wasn't having it. Even still, it didn't bother him; he found the man interesting, didn't mind his candor. The guy had a certain way of going about things, a grandfatherly way. He seemed to be compassionate and caring, gave off a sense of authenticity that appealed to Bennett.

The two finally stood up to go their separate ways.

"Do you come to this park often?" Bennett asked.

"You know, it's funny, even though the church is down the street, I never stopped here before. Passed it thousands of times but always took Jade to the park in Mt. Clemens since it's closer to home." He held up his finger. "You might not believe this but when I left this morning to come down to the church, I felt a pressing urge to bring Jade here, like God was telling me to do it."

"Hmm," Bennett nodded, thinking he was confusing his own intuition with the voice of God, a common mistake of the Ego.

"Maybe God wanted me to pray with you. Can I do that?"

Bennett didn't want to, seeing it as a waste of time, as supporting the superstition.

"Sure," he said.

The minister bowed his head. "Dear Lord, thank you for your love and compassion, your grace, your son, Jesus. Please reveal yourself to this man, please heal his ailments, both physical and spiritual, please..."

His voice faded into obscurity as Bennett's mind drifted elsewhere, considering the things he would do with the remainder of his day: go home, roast the pumpkin seeds he'd extracted the night before, and get ready for dinner with Sara and Leon.

"Amen," the minister said.

"Amen."

Bennett drove back home, listening to his XTC album *Skylarking* for the umpteenth time, thinking about the conversation with Jerome and the words of Ecclesiastes. He understood the need for some people to make up stories, to foster any semblance of meaning in their lives no matter how superfluous, to tell themselves certain ideas were true because without them life appeared hopeless. He believed that was the draw of religion, the thing that kept the masses perpetually enslaved. It was the fear of death, the fear of the unknown, the fear of fear. Without fear, nobody would have converted to most, if not all, of the dopey and unfounded convictions people deemed sacred. The primary purpose of the major religions in the world is to deny death, he figured, which they accomplish through the promise of an all-loving deity who prepares an afterlife of pleasure for the believer. As he was repeatedly told as a child, unfathomable joy awaits the herd while unrelenting suffering is the destiny of the unbeliever. Bennett related to the fear of death, just not to the point that it allowed him to embrace shoddy logic and delusion while retaining a sense of intellectual integrity. He wasn't fond of the notion of eternal annihilation, the obliteration of his own existence, returning to the state of "nothingness" that each individual arose from. It didn't suit his fancy. Atheism wasn't any more enjoyable than were his doubts about the supernatural claims of North Korea's latest dictator. But being rational and admitting uncertainties also didn't make him feel utterly worthless. He judged the alternative to be even worse: existing forever and ever, without ceasing, even against one's own wish to die.

[156]

He walked into his apartment, thinking about one observation in particular. It was that some people feared death so much, were so worked up by the idea of annihilation, that not only did they literally *do anything* to ensure their survival in *this life*, they also *believed anything* to ensure it in the *next*.

"What a strange response to death," he said, rubbing Mya's head. "What do you think, Mya? Have you lost any sleep over whether or not you're going to heaven?"

He stepped over to his bookshelf to return his old Bible and upon doing so, accidentally opened it to the front inside cover where a note was jotted:

My dear Bennett,

May the Lord continue to guide you as a loving husband, partner, and father, and may you lead this family in his holy ways. Your wife forever,

Lucia

P.S. Happy 10th Anniversary!!!

Chills washed over his body. His wife gave him this Bible in 1987 as an anniversary present; he was already deeply skeptical then, though he had known how to hide it. 1987 felt like another lifetime, so much had changed in the thirty-one years since. Even though he felt wiser, at bottom he didn't feel like he'd personally changed that much over the years. For a long time it worried him, especially after his divorce, after that morning on the MacArthur Bridge, after he quit the mortgage firm

[157]

and Angel left him. In many ways, he ruminated, it was those animals in his life during the past nineteen years—Shiva, Darwin, and Mya—that kept him going. Their loyalty and companionship outlasted any relationship he'd ever shared with another being, even an imaginary one. Perhaps I'm a failure by some standards, he concluded, but at least for the most part I learned to enjoy it.

He roasted pumpkin seeds, drenching them in butter and salt, whistling "The Man Who Sailed Around His Soul" by XTC. He called Sara to find out what time he should come by. She told him six thirty. It was just after three now. He decided to do some writing, maybe give his book another shot. He sat down at his café table, brainstorming, chain smoking his Marlboros. At last he settled on a premise.

His story would take place a hundred million years in the past, on another planet in the Milky Way galaxy where intelligent life similar to human beings once existed. Like modern humans, these intelligent beings were on the frontiers of space exploration. As it happened, they were "only" twelve light-years from earth, the closest Goldilocks planet they had yet discovered. They eventually developed the technology to send a machine, similar to a robot, through deep space to investigate the mystery planet. Half a century later, the robot reached earth. What would it find? Everyone on the home planet waited anxiously as the robot touched down and sent images of its terranean exploits back to the pioneers. To their astonishment, the aliens indeed found a planet beaming with life, creatures with bony structures, evolved with equipment for vision, hearing, communication, etc. To their great disappointment, however, the entire earth was ruled not by intelligent beings like themselves but monstrous lizards: the dinosaurs.

Bennett dwelt on his story, considering the plausibility of his account, fascinated by the scientific discoveries that made his premise entirely possible if not even likely. He knew there were hundreds of known planets within their respective star's habitable zone, possibly billions or trillions more. Undoubtedly, whatever beings may have existed on any such planet even fifty million years ago, it seemed unlikely that their civilization still remained. After all, extinction was the outcome for some 99.9% of species that scientists believe once roamed the earth. Even if other Goldilocks planets contained intelligent life, what were the odds of humans locating them, or vice versa, while both species were in the prime of their existence? Would humans still be around in fifty or a hundred million years, the average lifespan of a species being 1-10 million years? He didn't think the distant future looked too promising.

He realized he was digressing over insignificant details as he often did. He wrote a few paragraphs, scribbled them out, re-wrote and revised them, still unhappy with the result, finally giving up. It was almost six thirty anyway. He got dressed, putting on Erwin's old suit jacket, placed his shepherd's pie and pumpkin seeds in a bag, told Mya he'd be home soon enough, and walked downstairs to Sara's apartment.

"Bennett!" she said, opening the front door. "C'mon in! What did you bring?"

He noted that her apartment reeked of pot. "Made my 'World Famous Bennett Shepherd's Pie' and roasted pumpkin seeds!"

"Oh my god, you shouldn't have! I made plenty of food. Here, let me take your jacket."

He walked in and set his things down. Leon was standing in the kitchen, puffing on a blunt.

"Hey Bennett," he said, reaching out to shake hands.

Bennett reciprocated. "Hi Leon. How've ya been'?"

"I've been fine." He extended the weed to Bennett. "You?"

"Oh, no thanks. Doin' alright, had a rough couple of weeks but things have been goin' good the last day or so. It's weird actually."

"How so?" Sara asked, removing steaks from the oven.

"It's hard to explain, I think it's almost like being buzzed. I have this strange perspective on life, like I don't really give a fuck about anything anymore, but it's not depressing, it just 'is.' No good or bad, everything's very monotone..."

Leon looked puzzled, his face affirming the thought: Man, I'm high.

"Gee, don't get too cheerful on us," Sara said.

Everyone sat down at the table when the food was set. They ate, drank, chatted away. Bennett told Sara and Leon about the story he wanted to write.

"That's kinda cool, I guess," Leon opined. "I got an idea. What if that whole meteor that crashed into the earth or whatever and killed off the dinosaurs, what if that was actually a missile or somethin' sent by the aliens. What if they killed the dinosaurs, what if—"

"Yeah, I dunno," Bennett interrupted, "now you're turning it into the typical blockbuster. Big budget, silly script. Hey Leon, I've been meaning to ask you..."

"What's that?"

"What *did* you ever do with that sixteen dollars?"

He looked at Sara. "The sixteen dollars? Oh, right, that... Um..."

"You didn't do anything with it like I told ya too, did ya?"

"I did but..."

Sara broke out laughing. "He gave it to me! I made those cookies with it!"

"Chocolate chip..."

"Yep!"

"Not exactly what I had in mind but... Those *were* delicious."

The evening wore on, wine accompanying dinner, desert, and more wine. Bennett told them about the minister at the dog park.

"Wait, so you go up to dog parks and watch people with their dogs?" Leon asked, clumsily sipping his glass. He bumped Sara's elbow and joked, "Maybe that's how Bennett picks up pussy."

"Very funny," Bennett said, drunk and grinning. "And what would you know?"

Sara pounded the table. "I hate that word!'"

"Pussy?" they questioned. "What's wrong with the word 'pussy'?"

"Ah, stop!"

[161]

"Old man, I bet I know more about pussy than you do!" Leon said.

"Please!" Bennett chortled. "You know, it's funny though, I got the most pussy in my life in my forties and fifties. Who would've thought? There was one span when I dated five women whose name started with the letter K, almost all in a row—Kendra, Karen, Kylie, Krystal, and Kelsey."

Sara left to use the bathroom with a disgusted look on her face.

"So Leon," Bennett said, changing his tone, "you and Sara gettin' serious, eh? Might be movin' in together, I hear?"

He was slurring his words though he couldn't tell. He knew he was drunk, however, as soon as he asked Leon this question. Typically he would have reminded himself beforehand, 'It's none of my business.'

"Yeah," Leon said, rolling his eyes.

It caught Bennett by surprise, giving him the inkling that Leon was more or less acting out of obligation.

"She's in a tough spot," he continued. "I said I would try to help. She's a good person."

"She is. That's awfully nice of you though. Gotta be careful ya don't rush things, ya know? Take that as a tip."

Sara walked back into the kitchen. "What'cha guys talkin' about now?"

"Oh, nothing," Leon answered. "We were just talkin' about your artwork."

"Which one?"

"The one over here," Bennett said, "with the yellow swirls over

[162]

those objects. Are those supposed to be buildings?"

And on the night went. Willow Lane didn't allow soliciting, even on Halloween, so there were no trick-or-treaters. Everyone ate and drank too much, talking, laughing, celebrating the holiday. They discussed authors and books they enjoyed and played rummy, which Bennett wasn't too good at. His attention wandered to and fro on his upcoming trip to Texas, on seeing his family again. They would be together for the first time in years. His mind's eye visualized trick-or-treating with his children, passing out candy, carving pumpkins, holding his little girl on a hayride, taking Eugene through his first haunted house. It made him think of the closing line in a Woody Allen flick he'd seen on TV a week or so earlier: Is a memory something you have or something you've lost? To him they seemed gone forever, past lives only persisting on as abstractions inside a vanishing lump of goo, the peculiarity of conscious reflection. Soon it would all be lost.

"Bennett, you okay?" Sara asked.

"Huh? Oh, uh, yeah," he said, his eyes fluttering, struggling to stay open. It was late and they were wasted. "I gotta go home now. Goodnight everyone." So he left.

XII.

Autumn blues

He woke up the next morning and decided he would visit the Frederik Meijer Gardens and Sculpture Park in Grand Rapids, about a two hour drive from his apartment. He left around noon and arrived shortly after two. He invited Sara but she had school so he went by himself. It was a calm ride there as he basked in the tranquility and beauty of autumn's stain on nature, driving with his window halfway down, the temperature in the low 60's, the sun shining in all its glory. It was Angel who first showed him the exhibit, a large botanical garden with an outdoor art display, constructions large and small, abstract and realistic, made from wood and bronze and everything in between. He'd visited the place many times after they broke up, though many years had passed since his last visit. He surmised this would probably be his final opportunity to go.

He walked along the path admiring the various works, his favorites including the twenty-four foot tall bronze "American Horse" by sculptor Nina Akamu, the project commissioned of Leonardo da Vinci five centuries earlier; da Vinci was never able to complete it. He was particularly fascinated by its massive testicles, with their fine detail, and the muscle impressions, perfect in form. He was also fond of "Cabin Creek" by Deborah Butterfield, another horse, made of wood and metal that appeared almost mechanical, and "Neuron" by Roxy Paine. Like its name describes, it is a giant neuron made from over 3,500 stainless steel rods and pipe that stands forty-one feet tall. He felt as if it summarized the past decade succinctly, the steel mill and its brain-deadening atmosphere he'd happily left behind.

He had to take periodic breaks to catch his breath throughout his tour. Coughing spasms, which appeared to have subsided over the last few days, assaulted him again and again. That's what it felt like, an assault. After a couple of hours, his misfortunes grew to include persistent bouts of dizziness, intensifying to the point that he determined it best to retreat and go home. The drive seemed long and difficult, his mind fixated on his heart while he tried to remain attentive to the road. Eventually, he began to relax, finding himself distracted by public radio, an interview with an astrophysicist, the subject: the anthropic principle.

"So, now that you've explained a little bit about that," the interviewer said, "can you say something about the differences between the strong and weak versions of the anthropic principle?"

"Sure. The strong anthropic principle is more controversial and less widely accepted than the weak version. The strong form basically looks around at all this apparent symmetry, the age of the Universe, its fundamental and extraordinarily precise physical constants, and concludes that the Universe is such a way so as to *necessitate* the development of intelligent life. You might say things are conditioned for us rather than us for them."

[165]

Bennett thought about the old minister, Jerome. He would like the strong anthropic principle.

"The weak anthropic principle," the astrophysicist continued, "states that this ostensible fine-tuning is to be expected, *regardless* of probabilities, if only because we are able to perceive it. In other words, a Universe that contains beings who can behold their existence is inevitably one that will appear suited to them; the observation must always be compatible with the observer. I should also like to add that given the manner in which our brains have evolved, we have a tendency to attribute intentionality where it's not exactly warranted."

"Mm-hmm. But the appearance of intelligent life is a rather odd feature, isn't it?" the interviewer pressed. "That we're even on a 'knife's edge,' as it is often said, at all?"

"Odd? To us, sure, but much of what we discover about the Universe through science seems odd. That's merely an opinion, not an objective fact. Think about it this way: assuming that life couldn't have emerged in a Universe under different circumstances is to pretend that one knows exactly how life emerged given our present laws. There's still a lot we don't yet know about this enormously complex Universe. That's what excites us as scientists, our jobs look pretty safe," he concluded with a chuckle.

Bennett's mind wandered from the radio program to the famous teleological argument for God's existence put forth by William Paley in his seminal work *Natural Theology,* suggesting the oft-cited watchmaker analogy. For a long time as a Christian, Bennett thought this argument for God from nature's apparent fine-tuning was the strongest one available. It was when he was twenty-three years old that he discovered *The Origin of Species* and Charles Darwin's devastating refutation of Paley's teleology. Still, he couldn't help but ponder how or why animate matter, much less a Universe, should exist in the first place. He believed this was an unsolvable conundrum, the ongoing drive of intelligent beings, a perpetual question, one humans will fight over until their extinction, perhaps even leading to their extinction. Go figure. If there was a God, he pondered, this being *must* be asking the same question as well: *Why?* Why am *I* necessary? Even though he couldn't fathom what caused the fundamental physical constants to exist as they do, his rebuttal to religious charlatanism was always the following: "*What on earth makes you think religion is best suited to address this mystery?*"

When he arrived home his chest started bothering him again, the dizzy spells returning. He tried to sleep it off but couldn't elude the anxiety. "Am I dying *now?*" he wondered aloud to Mya. He ultimately ruled against his disinclination to see Doctor Fischer and drove to the hospital. On the way he stopped at the bank and withdrew his money, all ten grand. When he arrived at the cardiology department he was informed that Doctor Fischer was out of town for the remainder of the week, that he would have to see his partner, Doctor Abboud. He agreed and waited in the lobby, his chest throbbing, his breathing strained, growing more impatient by the

[167]

minute. Finally, a nurse appeared in the doorway.

"Mr. Shepherd?"

The nurse led him into a small room where he waited some more for the doctor to appear. When Doctor Abboud walked in, he became entranced by her voluptuous features, her tall and meaty stature outfitted in a short black skirt revealing beautiful, long, tan legs. His eyes admired them intently.

"Mr. Shepherd, I don't have all day," she said in a rich accent. "What is wrong?"

He snapped out of his fantasy. "Oh— I—uh..." He explained his symptoms, his visit with Doctor Fischer weeks earlier after his heart attack, and she ran some tests, took his blood. He told her about his financial situation, that he had nearly ten grand in hand and would pay for whatever treatment he could receive.

"Mr. Shepherd, it's not looking good," she said. "You shouldn't even be driving, really. You desperately need a VAD."

"A VAD?" he asked.

"Yes, a Vascular Assist Device. It pumps blood to your heart."

"You mean have open heart surgery?"

"Yes, that's what we do for people who are not eligible for a transplant."

"Shit, doc," he said, scratching his head, "how much does that cost?"

"Uh, it's hard to say, I don't deal with that."

"Ball park figure?"

"Very high."

"Upwards of ten, fifteen grand?"

She nodded.

Bennett threw a brief tantrum, coughed up what he felt like were his intestines, calmed down, got a prescription for a few additional medications, and left. He drove to the pharmacy, filled his scripts, and then went home.

"Try to relax and not do any strenuous activity," he scoffed on his way. "Yeah, that's easy for you to say."

He moped around in his apartment for the remainder of the day, feeling hollow. He placed the ten grand in a shoe box, on the top shelf in his closet, next to the box of letters from Eugene. He lit a cigarette but couldn't handle it so he threw it out along with the rest of the pack, done with them *for good* this time. He watched *The Hobbit* trilogy on TV which lasted until the wee hours of the night, then dug through his books for something that seemed appealing. He looked at his Christopher Hitchens collection, thought about the legendary old Hitch, how he also died of a terminal illness seven years earlier, like himself, at the age of sixty-two.

"I must remain valiant."

He pulled out an encyclopedic text on insects he owned, an enthralling work full of detailed descriptions on a variety of invertebrates, complete with exquisite photographs. Reading about different species of termites and the giant meticulous structures they build as colonial groups, an army of mindless "robots" modified by

[169]

evolution to design elaborate systems for nesting and farming, he was reminded of the human body, itself an elaborate structure designed by trillions of mindless individual cells. In some sense, he contemplated, the body is a cell-nest, a habitat for infinitesimal "organisms" on whose behalf it is "we" act upon, his brain confounded by the notion. Again he thought about the passage in Ecclesiastes he'd read the day before, the one that says, *"For that which befalleth the sons of men befalleth beasts; even one thing befalleth them: as the one dieth, so dieth the other; yea, they have all one breath; so that a man hath no preeminence above a beast: for all is vanity."* Indeed, he concluded, in many respects we are *not* all that different from insects.

He slept terribly that night, having awful, nonsensical nightmares from which he woke up sweating, coughing, in search of his inhaler. When morning arrived, he got out of bed, turned on his coffee maker, and wrote down the fragments he could recall.

He was standing in the foyer of the house he and Lucia once shared. There was silence except for a thunderstorm howling outside and rain clashing against the window. The house appeared dark and empty, lit only by candlelight. Making his way into the kitchen, a string of candles atop the counter, beer bottles sprawled about everywhere, he turned and saw two silhouette figures standing in the hallway leading to his bedroom, emerging into the flickering light. It was his children. They were teenagers.

"Was it worth it, dad?" his son asked.

"Yeah," Sophia mimicked, "was it worth it?"

The candles blew out and everything turned dark. That's when he woke up.

After Bennett finished writing in his notebook, he walked over to the coffee pot, poured himself a cup, and sat down in his recliner, Mya beside him as usual. Physically, he still felt like rubbish; getting out of bed had been a struggle. He meditated on his dreams, the life experiences that still haunted him. His train of thought led him back to his childhood, playing baseball with his siblings, getting into trouble with friends. In some ways, it seemed like only yesterday.

The sun slowly emerged from the morning fog until it burned intensely over clear skies. It looked like a pleasant November day but he was intent on remaining put, his chest feeling vulnerable to aches and palpitations. He sulked for a while on the couch, crooning tunes he thought up in his head, songs he termed the "Autumn Blues," an apt description for the mood he was in. As he began to gradually drift back asleep, the phone startled him.

"Hello?"

"Hey Bennett, just wanted to check up on ya, say hi." It was Jon from Virginia.

"Hey Jon. I've been meaning to call you."

"Did you figure out when you're comin' down?"

"Mm-hmm." Bennett walked over to his calendar. "I'm gonna leave on the thirteenth. It's about a ten hour drive from Ferndale to Colonial Heights. I figured I can make it in a day."

"You sure you'll feel up to it?"

"Yeah," he replied, coughing, "excuse me." He cleared his throat. "I think so."

"You talk to Sam and Marcy since we last spoke?"

"Uh-huh. I'm gonna stay with you 'til the following Sunday, the eighteenth, then I'll drive to Marcy's. She said to come down whenever."

"That's gonna be a helluva lotta drivin'. You plannin' on taking I-85 through Atlanta?"

"Yep. About what, a twenty hour drive?"

"Yeah, that's over 1,300 miles," Jon said. "When my pops used to drive us down there back in the day as kids he'd make it in seventeen and a half."

"I'll probably spend the night somewhere in Alabama. Get to Tomball sometime on Monday."

"Sounds great. And you're gonna see Eugene and Sophia then?"

"Yeah, talked to the two of 'em last week. Gene's flight comes in on the twentieth. I can't wait to see them."

"I can't wait to see you, cousin."

Bennett began to feel better. "Me too."

After he finished talking, he reclined in his chair and closed his eyes. It felt surreal that he was leaving in scarcely over a week. He didn't have any idea if he would ever come back to Detroit. He rubbed Mya's head while she rested on his lap, unsure if he would bring Mya on the journey. He didn't want to leave her behind but he also didn't know what to do with her, the car being no place for a cat. Whenever he transported Mya in her cage, like on the number of occasions when he moved, after about five miles she always ended up vomiting. He couldn't imagine putting her in a cage for a two thousand mile bumpy ride. She would hate it. He thought about giving her to Sara or Jasmine. Either one of them would make an excellent owner.

His eyes once again began to drift off and he found himself sitting in his living room, talking to Sara about Mya.

"How heavy is it if she's standing on bricks?" she asked.

"What?" He returned to his senses, realizing he'd begun dreaming, halfway in that transition of being awake and asleep, a so-called 'wake dream.'

He closed his eyes. Again the phone rang.

"Hello?"

"Bennett!" It was Marty.

"Oh, hey Marty." Bennett wished he hadn't answered it.

"I was callin' to give you the info for your going away party!"

"Oh."

"You didn't forget about it, did ya? I told ya to invite people, remember?"

"Yeah, I remember... but how am I supposed to invite people if I dunno where to tell them to go?"

"That's what I'm callin' ya for! I decided we're gonna have it at that bar where your friend works, The Showcase."

"Oh, okay. Great." Bennett tried to muster excitement in his tone, if only to give the appearance of gratitude. Truthfully, he didn't find the idea of a going away party very appealing. He could only imagine what it would be like, everyone pretending to be sad over his departure while secretly pitying him, whispering behind his back about his terminal illness:

"He doesn't even seemed phased."

"He's like a statue or—or a zombie!"

"Poor guy."

"Okay then," Marty said, "November twelfth, eight P.M., at The Showcase. Let people know!"

He agreed to everything Marty said, hung up the phone, massaged his torso, feeling more pain. He wondered how he would make it to Texas if the heart palpitations did not cease, a tightness in his chest growing more persistent and unforgiving with each beat. Popping another one of his pills, he diverted his attention to more important matters, contemplating whom he should invite to his party. He didn't have a lot of friends. He *knew* a lot of people but the ones he counted as friends, those he liked well enough and had a history with, the kind he would *want* at his party, were few and far between.

"Dave and Fred?" he asked Mya, who ignored him, blissfully

napping on his knees. "Nah, they're not really friends. But ah, screw it, who else do we have to invite?" He ran through various names in his head: Sara, Leon, Jasmine, but she'd already be there, Marty and the guys from poker would be there, hmm... Were those the only people he liked?

"Wow, Mya," he said. "I've managed to get by fairly independently, I'd say. Either that or I really am a total loser."

Bennett didn't do too much the rest of the day. He didn't call anyone either. He watched TV, made a plate of pasta salad, slept on and off, didn't have any memorable dreams to record. He tried to do more writing but nothing satisfied him. As the night wore on, his chest pains eased though sleep remained elusive. He woke up at one point, sweating profusely, noting the clock read 4:23 A.M., then coughed, cleared his throat, and resumed snoring.

XIII.

The cross we bear

"Born on March 6, 1956, at 4:23 A.M." said a female voice. "Six pounds, two ounces."

That's my birthday, Bennett thought, realizing that once again he was in a delivery room, his father standing next to his mother situated comfortably on a bed, his older siblings also present. Unseen, he watched from the corner.

"He's beautiful," his mother said, taking the newborn in her arms.

"That's your baby brother, Bennett Raymond Shepherd," said his father, looking down at the two small children beside him.

"Daddy," the little girl said, "why's he all red?"

"It's blood," said the boy.

"Ew, gwoss."

"You're going to do wonderful things one day," his mother whispered to the child, her eyes wet from tears of joy.

Bennett glanced towards the end of the room where the entrance was and noticed a bar through the doorway. He thought it peculiar that an open bar would be directly across from the delivery room, much less in a maternity ward. He exited and realized he was standing in The Showcase. Jasmine's eyes locked with his from behind the bar, arms stretched over the top, leaning towards him. A whiskey glass sat on a napkin beneath her.

"You gonna sit down? *This is your* party, ya know?"

Bennett took a seat, looking around, feeling strange. The place was empty.

"This is my party?" he asked. "What do you mean?"

"You're going away party! What else did ya think, silly?"

"Jazz, are you fuckin' with me? Nobody's here."

"Bennett, what in God's name are you talking about? Are you already drunk? *Look* at everyone!" She pointed to the other side of the bar. Now anyone he could ever remember was gathered around the pool table and the dart board, sitting in the few booths available, chatting, laughing, drinking. He looked to his right. There was karaoke on the dance floor, his father in the center, holding a microphone, singing a familiar tune, "We've Only Just Begun" by The Carpenters.

"So much of life ahead..."

Bennett turned back around.

"See?"

"What're we celebrating? The fact that I'm leaving?"

"No, goofball," she said, nudging his arm. "We're celebrating *your life.*"

He stared at her disinterested. "I feel sick." He stood up, wobbling back and forth. He half staggered, half floated his way through the bar, aiming for the bathrooms near the back exit.

"Benny boy!" someone yelled, grabbing onto his shirt as he stumbled by. He looked down. It was his older brother, in a booth with

[177]

his other siblings, Marcy and Sam.

"Sit down, chill out," Marcy said. "Are you high at your own party, Bennett?"

"That would make two of us then," Jack said.

Bennett sat down, bewildered, dizzy, the dreamy room beginning to spin. Gazing beneath the table where his legs disappeared into darkness, he became seized by the notion that he might slide off the seat. In fact, he *had* slid down a ways. Digging his nails into the fabric and trying with all his might, he propped himself back up, realizing in the process that the material of the bench felt almost like linen, the fractal pattern on it familiar. As soon as the thought penetrated his sense of identity and surrounding, he found that he *was* sitting on his bed, in his childhood room, the covers decked out in a psychedelic design, his choice style as a teenager.

"What is this filth, Bennett? Where did you get it? You have some explaining to do to your mother and I!"

He looked up and saw his old man towering over him. It didn't occur to him how he got here, more concerned with his father's face, scrunched up with brows slanted inward to indicate seriousness or something. His father was holding up a pornographic magazine.

"My son isn't a pervert!" he screamed, magazine rolled up in his hand, pointing it at his son. "This is a Christian household and we will follow the Lord! I will have none of this in my house!" His cheeks were as red as a Vermillion Flycatcher.

Bennett's mother walked into the room, trying to appease the situation.

"Why can't you be more like your brother?" his father continued. "Jack is going to be an all-American athlete, he's always on the highest honor rolls, and you—all you do is screw off with your friends, getting into trouble, reading this garbage!" Finishing his lecture, he glanced at his wife and stormed out.

"Ben, honey," his mother said softly, sitting down on the bed and embracing him. "You need to ask Jesus for forgiveness. If you're feeling tempted or struggling with something, you can always come to us. The Devil's ways are cunning, don't try to fend him off by yourself."

Bennett felt ashamed, embarrassed, dirty. That's when the dream ended.

He remained in his bed listening to a down pouring rain outside. He wanted to get up to record his dream before he forgot it but he couldn't muster the strength. The clarity of his account evaporated after a few moments. He didn't feel physically ill, nor his chest bound in knots as he had experienced previously. Emotionally, however, he felt drained, exhausted, depressed. As he lay there, Mya resting at his feet, he recalled what his mother used to tell him whenever he would be sad as a young boy.

"Bennett, sweetie," she'd say, "there's only one way to cure a sad heart: go out of your way to do something nice for someone else. It'll always make you feel better."

He contemplated what nice things he could do until an idea came to mind. Jumping out of bed, he fed Mya her canned turkey with cheese, showered, took his medications, pulled his leather jacket over his head because he lacked an umbrella, and walked out the door.

He decided he would go to Ron King Books, an independent book store that specializes in used and rare books, and buy something for Sara. He lived a block away from one of the store's three locations but instead went to the main store, the original site which housed a much larger collection of books. It was in downtown Detroit, no more than a fifteen minute trip. He drove his Mercury through the drizzle down Woodward, past the Fox Theater, past the stadium and arena where the Tigers and Red Wings play, and turned right onto West Lafayette. His car splashed a puddle the size of a small pool as he skidded to a stop, arriving at the bookstore.

When he entered, he recalled how much he enjoyed coming to this store in the past and regretted how little he had taken advantage of it. The building consisted of four levels above ground and a basement, packed from top to bottom with rows of tall bookshelves. He spent a while getting lost, wandering through the stacks, the vast expansion of unique literature, inhaling the satisfying aroma, entirely unsure where he should begin browsing. He knew Sara liked fiction novels, books that were educational as well as anything involving art therapy. He poked around and found her an art therapy book, then, continuing to inspect each aisle, moseyed into the New Age section. He'd seen many

[180]

of the same books in Jasmine's house years ago. Even though Sara wasn't a believer, he figured maybe he could find something she'd appreciate in this section too. He perused the wide selection, unable to locate anything respectable. Suddenly, an author caught his attention: Robert Anton Wilson. The name stuck out to him because he remembered Sara saying, after he noted how she signed her artwork, that her last name was Wilson too. Sara Wilson, Robert Anton Wilson, perhaps there is significance to it, he teased himself.

The book he picked up was *Cosmic Trigger: The Final Secret of the Illuminati,* an older-looking text from the '70s with interesting conspiratorial artwork on the cover, a rainbow, a few orbiting moons, and a pyramid with an eye on the top. He opened it up, his internal comic prepared to mock whatever gibberish he expected the author to espouse. Two hours later, he was *still* reading, absorbed, unable to set it down. He thought the book was complete nonsense and yet it was so beautifully written that he couldn't help but wonder if perhaps the author was onto something. It was a mixture of science, philosophy, and mysticism, interwoven with an autobiographical narrative that boasted *a lot* of LSD.

"I definitely have to get this for Sara," he said.

When he left the bookstore, the rain had ceased and the sun was already beginning its descent into the evening horizon. Holy shit, he thought, I spent five hours in there! He got into his car and drove home, engaged in silent conservation with himself.

I think Sara's gonna love this book.

[181]

Feelin' better?

Yeah, I do. Mom was right.

She always was.

Well, not *always*.

This book is a mind fuck.

How did you get by so long without knowing of such a book?

I dunno. That's sad though, isn't it? We go our whole lives unaware of some great book or wonderful piece of art, some special idea, some extraordinary person. It remains totally non-existent to us, in *our* Universe. And yet someone else can think that person or idea was the best thing ever conceived.

It makes you wonder, what else have you missed out on, eh?

I mean, yeah, but that's also what makes life truly marvelous, worth living. Each day is an opportunity to seek out whatever it is you find fulfillment in. There's always somethin' entirely foreign and new to learn, to understand, to enrich your experience...

His internal dialogue went on and on while he stalled out in rush hour traffic, cars beeping at one another, everyone in a frenzy to arrive at wherever it was they thought so urgently demanded their presence. Even that didn't get under his skin today. At last he returned to Willow Lane.

"What the hell..." he said upon entry. There were police cars outside, a fire truck and an ambulance. He parked, trying to get a glimpse of what was going on. He noticed people coming in and out of

[182]

Sara's place and raced towards the scene. A few officers turned around to prevent him from going any further.

"Get off me! I live upstairs!"

Neighbors stood outside observing the racket.

"Sir!" an officer said, getting up in his face. "You have to calm down!"

Bennett recognized the cop. It was the one who had knocked on his car window weeks earlier and threatened to cite him for public intoxication. The cop recognized him too.

"Can you tell me what's going on?" he asked, backing off. Over the officer's shoulder, he saw a stretcher being wheeled out of Sara's apartment. There she was, respirator attached to her face. "What the fuck! That's my neighbor! My friend! What happened?!"

The cop stepped to the side of the small crowd surrounding Sara's door and motioned for Bennett. He wanted to speak in private.

"Appears to be an overdose of something," he said. "Do you know anything about a drug problem she may have had?"

"A drug problem? No..."

"Marijuana? Pills? Anything like that?"

"What kind of pills?"

Another officer walked up and stood nearby.

"Clonazepam, right?"

"Looks like it," the other officer said.

From the corner of his eye, Bennett saw Leon pull up in his mother's SUV, swerving halfway into a parking spot, screeching his tires. He jumped out.

"No, she fuckin' did it, *didn't she?!*" he cried, running up to the blockade of police. "She fuckin' did it!"

"What did she do?" the offers inquired.

It took Leon a moment to get his words out.

"*What* did she do?!" Bennett asserted.

"I—I broke up with her ye—yesterday," Leon said, out of breath. "Today we—we got into an argument. She told me she was goin'— goin' to take all of her pills. She said she didn't wanna live anymore. She told me she took them and I called 911 because I—I believed her." He continued crying.

"That was a very smart decision, kid," the officer said.

"Leon, where'd she get clonazepam?"

"I think she got 'em like a week ago from her doctor." He wiped his eyes, still failing to fully get a grip on himself. "Is she gonna be alright?"

"I think so," the officer said. "She's very lucky you called us when you did."

"Is she goin' to the hospital right up the road?" Bennett asked.

"Yeah, Royal Oak."

Bennett ran to his car and drove off, leaving Leon and the police officers behind, racing towards the hospital. He zigzagged through traffic, chest pains beginning to aggravate him again but his attention focused solely on Sara. The palpitations intensified, his legs ached as if swollen. "Steady, old man," he murmured, slowing down as he approached a red light. A few times he felt like he might pass out but he wouldn't allow himself to. His thoughts were jumbled, his nerves in shock. *What the hell was she thinking?* What'd she need pills for? Sara sees a psychiatrist?

At last he arrived at the hospital and sprinted to the emergency room, all too familiar as he'd been in the same hospital to see Doctor Abboud, the same hospital they rushed *him* to after his heart attack.

"I'm here to see Sara Wilson," he told the woman behind the lobby desk. "She just came in, uh, benzo' overdose or somethin'?"

"One moment," the woman said, looking at some papers and walking away briefly. "Sir," she said, "you can have a seat until the gastric suction is finished."

He looked at her puzzled.

"They have to pump her stomach. Then she'll be administered an IV to get her fluid levels back to normal. We may need to keep her overnight depending on how high the toxicity in her blood is. We'll let you know as soon as you can go see her. Should only be a little bit now."

"Okay," he said, turning to find a seat.

"Excuse me, are you her father by any chance?" the woman asked.

"Oh no. A friend."

He walked over to a chair, his thoughts whizzing by a dozen per second. Sadness and anger overcame him as he considered the possibility that Sara could have died. It made him want to break down right then and there. He maintained his composure, however, reminiscing on his father at the psychiatric hospital the day of his mother's death. He felt as lost as his father appeared then: a complete mess, in a daze, rife with shock. He was reminded of Jack. Jr., who was not so lucky to survive an overdose. What drove Sara to this point? How could I be so *blind*? What did *Leon* do? Leon is a hero, he thought. He saved her life.

He didn't have to wait too long until a nurse came out to inform him that Sara was doing okay, resting, that he could go and see her. Even still, he lost his sense of time waiting in the lobby. It seemed like he'd sat there for hours. While he waited, he invited Dave and Fred to his going away party. He didn't want to call them so he sent out multiple text messages (not being very fluent in technology, it took him a minute).

He followed the nurse into Sara's room. She lay on a bed, her face pale, asleep, hooked up to an IV.

"Once we get her fluid levels normalized, she'll be free to go," the nurse said. "In the meantime, she needs some rest."

"Oh, I'm not her father," he replied as she walked away.

He approached Sara's bed and pulled up a seat. He examined her, his sadness and anger replaced by yearning and compassion. He put his head into his hands and began to cry.

"Bennett?"

He looked up at Sara. She wore a gentle, weary smile.

"What happened?" she asked.

"I thought I lost you," he said, struggling to speak. "You overdosed."

[186]

"Oh." She sighed a deep breath, a look of disgust overcoming her. "Did Leon call 911?"

"I think so. He may have saved your life. Tell me what's goin' on... Just the other day, everything—"

"Bennett," she said. "I've been depressed for a while now. It feels like I've been fighting it my whole life. I tried to hang in there. Meeting Leon felt like the greatest thing for me. Then he broke up with me yesterday, said I was pushing things on him too quickly, that I'm too unstable, that he doesn't really like me *like that*." She began to choke up.

"Leon may have saved your life..."

"He's still an asshole!"

"But what about the other people who care about you? What about me? I care about you more than you know. You've helped me so much these last few weeks. You've been more of a friend to me than I could've ever imagined I'd have during a time like this."

"Why, Bennett? Because I talk to you? Because I listen to you? Is that how shitty people are, that if you treat 'em like a human being you're seen as doing something extraordinary?"

"I only mean—"

"I like you a lot. You're a good person and a good friend but I'd be lying if I said your situation hasn't affected me. Your facing death and everything, it's made me do a lot of thinking about my own life, my own mortality. It hurts to think I'm gonna lose you, that you're gonna leave me soon."

Mucus, water, and oil ran down his cheeks, steadily falling onto his

[187]

shoes.

"Don't cry, Bennett," she said, wiping his face.

"I've only known you for a few weeks and yet it feels like I've known you for ages. I couldn't imagine having to go to your funeral. You're so young! You have your entire life before you! Remember what I said the other day at Telly's?"

Tears filled her eyes. "I know but I don't really wanna live anymore. What's an entire life of unrest, of unhappiness? I don't feel like I belong in this world. It's not for me. I don't want to be stuck in a dead end job, always struggling, always seeking the next plateau."

"I know," he said. "You wanna see the world like in that Steinbeck novel—travel, discover. But it takes time to get there. And you can't worry about me! I'm doin' fine..."

"How're you doin' fine?! You're dying!"

He thought about Jerome's words from earlier in the week. "You know I'm not religious but I once heard somethin' interesting. Everyone has a cross to bear. Each of us bears the cross of mortality. Everything, from the Universe to the stars, from ants to you and I, we all face the same thing in the end, we all face death. Bearing your cross means embracing it, accepting the fact that life is finite, that reality is only as good and worthwhile as you make it to be. It's coming to terms with the hardships and not losing your dignity in the process. Only then can you truly fulfill your purpose, your role, whatever niche it is that nature carved out for you when it granted you a space in existence."

[188]

"That sounds nice."

He didn't know if she meant it or not but he thought it sounded nice too, especially since he made it up on the spot.

"It makes sense up here," she said, pointing to her head. Then she placed her hand on her heart. "But not here. We're too evolved for our own good. Too self-aware."

"When did you start taking clonazepam?" he asked, changing the subject.

"About a week and a half ago, got 'em from a psychiatrist..."

"I didn't even know you were seeing one."

"It's not the kind of thing people typically *brag* about. I haven't been able to sleep lately. My thoughts race, I get anxious, worry about things, which is not like me. I don't like to worry about tomorrow. I have to keep my head in the present. That's the only way to stay sane. I figured they would help me sleep."

He gazed down, hurt over his friend's hopelessness. "Yeah... Hey, guess what?"

"Hmm?"

"I bought a couple of books for you today."

"You did?"

"Yeah. An art therapy one. And this other one called *Cosmic Trigger*. The author has the same last name as you. Wilson."

"Oh yeah? What's that about?"

"I dunno how to describe it exactly. Weird shit—conspiracy theories, UFOs, acid trips, philosophy, quantum physics."

[189]

"Sounds weird." Color was starting to return to her face. "I dunno if I can handle anything like that right now though."

"Understandable. Whenever you're ready for it."

"Sara!" a voice called from the doorway.

A woman ran in. She had an uncanny resemblance to Sara but appeared much older, older than her age actually was. She looked as if she had led a difficult life, merely surviving. Her face was red from crying.

"Hey mom..."

Bennett stood up. "Well, I'll leave you two alone."

"Thanks for coming, Bennett. It means a lot. I'll call you tomorrow."

He hugged her and departed.

Bennett damn near wept like an infant the entire ride home. He cried some more once he got inside his apartment, his eyes pressed in friendly orange fur, talking to his favorite therapist. She did what she was best at. She listened and purred. He deliberated in his head over what would have happened had he not been there to console Sara. Who did she have in her life? Her mother? She was like him in a lot of ways, an introvert, a free thinker, a cynic, a realist, a naturalist. While he digested the events of the day, he completely forgot to worry about his own ailments—his chest pains, fatigue, shortness of breath. At Mya's urging, he summoned the strength to get up and feed her though he didn't have much of an appetite himself. Once again he numbed his emotions with the mindless nonsense of television programming. The rain outside began again. He listened to it clash against the window

[190]

and lit incense Sara had given him days before, pondering whether he should call his children to say hello but it was too late. He shut off the TV after a while and sat there, staring at shadowy figures on the walls created by the moon's glow, replaying his conversation with Sara on the day before Halloween, the day they ate breakfast together, the day he ran into Marty at the grocery store.

"Maybe I'll realize all of my experiences on earth were only a fraction of reality," he heard himself say.

"Like all *this*, all of the things we perceive, they're only illusions, like Plato's shadow people?" she asked cheerfully, her speech fading back to into the recesses of his imagination.

He reflected on all the people he'd known, the people from his dream the prior night, when he dreamt he was at The Showcase for his going away party. He thought about those in his past who had long been dead: Jack Jr., his parents, friends, others he no longer knew, people around the world who passed over from this life to eternal oblivion at every second, many of them children, many of them sick, poor, lost to drug addiction, holding on to any chance that a better place awaited them. He knew otherwise, at least he was fairly certain, all of those lives deceived by a hope that earth was preparation for something greater, spared both disappointment and satisfaction when the cold truth of reality struck.

He considered people such as Sara, someone who wasn't sure if there was an afterlife and yet found existence so intolerable that the possibility of annihilation seemed like a preferable alternative. He was

[191]

convinced that he never possessed the courage to kill himself, even on that day twenty-one years earlier. It was all a ploy, a drama enacted by his brain to reveal the escape plan, the light at the end of the tunnel, to demonstrate the utter depravity he felt as the person he was at the time. He didn't think, in retrospect, that he could have actually gone through with it. But what about Sara? he speculated, staring at the creepy figures on his apartment walls, the actual illusions. She could have died. Did she really view life so callously?

"Life is so precious," he said to Mya, who curled up next to him. "I've been so lucky. *So* lucky. I don't have anything to complain about. My journey has been worth every moment. Every moment I still have is precious."

He didn't get much in the way of rest that night. He woke up shortly after noon, staggered to his recliner and turned on the TV to watch Sunday football. His chest ached as if someone had poured cement down his throat during the night, like something *hardened* inside. He lounged around, watching the early game, looking at his phone every other minute, anticipating Sara's call. After a couple of hours, it rang.

"Sara?" he answered enthusiastically.

"Hey Bennett, I'm home now. Well, not home—I'm at my mom's house. She insisted I stay with her for a few days, doesn't want me to be alone."

"In Hazel Park?"

"Yeah. You're more than welcome to come by. My mom's gonna be at work all day anyway, she told me to have someone over."

"She works on Sunday?"

"Yeah, at Country Girl, it's a restaurant over on—"

"I know where that is. Well, sure, I'll come visit."

"Only if you're not busy though..."

"Oh *shut up*, I'm not busy at all!"

She gave him directions to her mother's house. He showered, left out food for Mya, took his blood thinners, his pills for high blood pressure, the pill to prevent chest pains, and the array of other pharmaceuticals he'd been prescribed, then got into his car and drove to Hazel Park.

Sara's mother lived in a modest house, a little run down, comfortable enough for a small family. It was only about a five minute drive from Willow Lane. He embraced Sara when she came to the door, in her pajamas, still sporting her hospital wristband. She invited him in, offered him coffee and a seat on her mother's sofa. She looked much better than the previous evening, he surveyed. He handed her the books he'd bought for her. She glossed over the Wilson one and smirked.

"Looks trippy."

"Heh, yeah. So, uh, how're ya feelin'?"

"I'm feelin' better. My brain kind of feels like mush today. Yesterday is a big blur. I can't believe I actually took all those pills."

"How many did you take?"

[193]

"Around ten. But it was the mixing it with liquor that did me in."

"I can't understand why—"

"Me neither!" she blurted out. "I dunno what came over me... Everything with Tom and Leon... Of course, you... And me not knowing where I'll end up, here at my mom's, if I'll still be in school next year... It all got to me at once. It overwhelmed me."

"But you've never struck me as the type of person who worried over stuff like that."

"That's the thing, I've always kept myself busy so that I wouldn't *have* to think about bullshit like that. And yet once I got on that train of thought, I couldn't get off of it. It just barreled downhill."

"You talk to Leon since yesterday?"

"Nah, he's called a few times. I texted him to say I was okay and to thank him for calling 911... But I don't really want anything to do with him right now. I feel so used. Ugh."

"You know, when you had me over for dinner, I suspected somethin' was off with him."

"What'cha mean?"

"Well, I mentioned somethin' about you two moving in together and he kind of brushed it off, didn't seem that keen to it. I thought it was odd, given everything you had told me, I figured things were going well for you two."

"Yeah, so did I... but ya know what, Bennett? I thought some more about what you said to me, about finding happiness within myself, not depending on others for contentment. I think you're right. I feel like

[194]

today is a fresh start. No more relying on others the way I have. I'm going to make a conscious *effort to be happy*. It's like I have a new lease on life. I've lost like, the, uh—"

"Fear?"

"Right! I've lost the fear, whatever it was that held me back, fear of abandonment, insecurity, I dunno, the fear of losing."

They spent the whole afternoon together. Bennett felt relieved, emboldened, alive—he felt alive again, his fear of death gone, a feeling that the fear was always irrelevant in the first place, irrelevant to the present, the now. He told Sara about his older brother Jack, how he died of an overdose in '79.

"It was a speedball, heroin and coke."

"Oh my god... you've never told me about your older brother, that he died like that. That's horrible. And he was going to be a professional baseball player?"

"That's what everyone said when he was in high school. Yeah, it's a sad memory."

They played chess, talked about the hospital, its unpleasant smell, the nurses and doctors—some friendly, others not so much—his upcoming trip to Virginia and Texas. To his surprise, she was a very skilled chess player, beating him two out of three games.

"So what're you gonna do with Mya?"

He looked out the window pensively. "I've been thinking about that. I want you to have her. She loves you. You'd make a great mommy to her."

[195]

"Really? You're going to give me your cat?"

He sighed, scanning the floor, searching for the invincibility he felt moments ago. "I can't take her with me. I'd like to but that's no journey for a cat. And what happens when I get to Texas? My daughter wouldn't take her. *Definitely* not my brother or sister. I'm learning to take things one day at a time. I might come back but I can't plan that far ahead."

Thus it was settled. Sara would take his cat. When it came time to go, he hugged her, told her to call him and let him know how she was coming along.

"Oh yeah, one more thing," he said, turning around as he walked away. "My friend is having a going away party for me, a week from tomorrow, on the twelfth. It's gonna be at a place called The Showcase, in Warren."

"Okay," she said. "I'll come. What time?"

"Around eight, I think."

"But I'll see you sooner than that. I should be back at my place in a few days."

He waved goodbye and drove off.

It wasn't even two full days before Sara called, early on Tuesday morning, waking him from a heavy sleep.

"Ugh... H-Hello?"

"Hey, sorry to bother you."

He looked at the clock, rubbing his eyes. 12:11 A.M. "Uh, it's alright.

You okay?"

"My mother, oh my god, I want to *kill* her! I can't take it anymore. I hate asking people for favors like this but I wanted to know if it would be alright, if perhaps, um—"

"You wanna stay with me a few days?"

"Yes!" she said, breathing a sigh of relief.

"Sure, that'd be fine. You need a lift?"

"No, my friend can drop me off in the mornin'."

She appeared at his front door shortly after 10 A.M., a few bags of clothes in hand, a cigarette in her mouth, a Marlboro Special Blend 100.

"Come on in," he said, moving to the side. "You're smoking?"

"I couldn't help myself. My mom stresses me the fuck out. I'll probably smoke this pack and be done. Want one? I bought your kind."

"Nah, I quit last week actually. Couldn't handle 'em anymore."

She brought her things into his apartment. Mya greeted her with a couple of bunts to her leg. She bent down, looking at her soon-to-be-adopted cat. "Hi Mya... Bennett, we're gonna miss you so much!"

He glanced away.

"Hey, I'll be right back," she added. "I gotta grab some stuff from downstairs. Mind if I grab a few art supplies?"

"Not at all, make yourself at home."

Minutes later she returned from her apartment with a bag of materials, weed, and her bong.

"Whoa, cops didn't confiscate that stuff?"

"Nope. How could they?" She held up medical marijuana papers. "Legal in the state of Michigan. I keep this posted on my refrigerator." She plopped down on the couch with the bong between her legs. "Wanna toke up?"

He thought about it for a second, his lungs feeling weak, knowing it would probably aggravate them. "Sure, why not?" he answered, giving into the peer pressure that his internal dialogue had manufactured.

Sara lived with him for a total of seven days. She arrived at his apartment on November 6 and remained with him until he left town the following week. He enjoyed her company immensely. They grocery shopped together, she cooked his meals and painted him wonderful pictures; a beautiful crucifix she titled "The Cross We Bear," an empty cross hanging over a murky abyss. It made Bennett think of the painting "Nearer My God To Thee" by the infamous "Dr. Death," Jack Kevorkian. Sara's piece was like that except instead of a frightened man sliding down into a bottomless pit, clawing on to the walls of existence, her helpless figure was tied to a cross, his eyes closed peacefully, no expression on his face, the cross scraping the sides of the gulf as it slowly descended upon the glares of the dead below.

"Yeah, I can't lie, that Kevorkian piece inspired this one," she said. "Well, that and what you said to me in the hospital."

They spent many nights staying up late, talking about the great mysteries of existence, the mundane, the perplexing, the silly: What existed before the Big Bang? What is time? How did life emerge? Is there intelligence on other planets? What is consciousness? Can our morality ever save us? And on and on it went, the questions never ending—some more useful than others—the answers never satisfying.

Most nights Bennett would fall asleep in his recliner, Sara on the couch. The thought of sharing a bed never crossed their minds. Both would've considered the notion strange. She was like a daughter to him, he like a crazy uncle to her. He showed her the notebook of dreams he'd been recording. She asked him many questions about his past, his life in Tomball, The Woodlands, his experiences as a child, as an adult, his family, his girlfriends, his career as a coin minter, a metalworker, a loan officer, dozens of odd jobs in between, his pets, his friends, everything about his life. She found his stories fascinating.

"They had *the* best burgers," he said on one occasion. "Their Angus beef with caramelized onion and stacked sauce! Mmmm! My father always used to get that."

His chest pains didn't much improve, even with the plethora of medications he was taking. A couple of times whilst driving he felt like he was going to pass out. He started having Sara drive him around.

"Are you going to be okay on your trip? You're gonna be driving what, like fifteen hundred miles?"

"Two thousand. Yeah, I'll be okay. I'll pull over when I need to. If it takes a little longer to get there, that's okay. Usually I can settle myself down after a minute or two. Coffee helps keep me alert so long as I don't overdo it."

When Thursday arrived, Sara had to return to work at the thrift store. She dreaded the idea, knowing she would have to confront Leon.

"It won't be that bad. We hardly ever worked together before."

"Well, you have my number if you need to call me for anything, to shoot the shit or whatever," Bennett tried to console her.

He gave her his spare apartment key that he kept in his kitchen junk drawer. "You don't have to worry if I'm home. Come and go whenever you please."

He began packing his things as the thirteenth approached. He decided he would leave his furniture behind as he had no way of transporting it and hiring a moving truck was out of the question. He told Sara she could have whatever wouldn't fit into his car. It was bittersweet. He very much looked forward to seeing his family, Sophia and Eugene, long forgotten friends, and though he knew he'd be in better care down there, he was sad about deserting Michigan, his home for the past twenty-six years. I'll be back here, he told himself.

Finally, the day of his going away party arrived.

XIV.

Goodbye, farewell

Her eyes fluttered until the fuzzy objects around her became clear. Light beamed through the shades, illuminating a spectacular autumn day. The TV was on: "Today's going to be absolutely gorgeous! Highs in the 70's for the next few days!" a man's voice declared. Sara yawned and looked around. Bennett slept in his recliner across the room dispensing a loud, calm snore, as did Mya, curled up on Sara's feet at the end of the couch. Today's our last day together, she reflected, tomorrow he leaves. It was a disheartening thought but she didn't want to spend her final day with Bennett in a lousy mood so she got up and began cooking breakfast. I'm going to make this a wonderful day for him, she decided.

He woke up to bacon sizzling on the stove, freshly brewed coffee, toast in the toaster, the smells of an elegant brunch.

"What's this?" he asked, standing up, stretching. "The Last Breakfast?"

"Take a seat," she said. "You looked like *you* were sleepin' good... man, do you snore!"

"Oh I was, I was having a ridiculous dream," he said as he walked to the refrigerator, still rubbing his eyes.

"What was it about?"

He reached for the milk. "Hmm... Actually, I don't remember anything about it." He took a swig from the carton and looked at the label. One percent.

"Ew, you're drinking milk by itself?"

He put the carton back in the refrigerator and turned to her, wiping away his mustache. "Yep, been a lifelong drinker. But I prefer two percent."

He sat down at his café table and the two ate breakfast together. She made eggs, bacon, and pancakes, with toast on the side, and set jelly, butter, syrup, powered sugar, and orange juice on the table for Bennett to help himself.

"So today's the day," she said, glancing at him across the table while he stuffed his mouth full of pancakes. "Your party tonight and then tomorrow you leave."

He stopped chewing, his gaze turning solemn as he stared off into space.

She waved her hand to snap him out of his stupor. "Bennett? Hello?"

"Oh, yeah, um, sorry... It's hard to believe I already leave tomorrow... feels weird."

"You know it was a month ago yesterday that we first met on the bus?"

His eyes widened. "Only a month? Sheesh!"

"So what's your plan for the day?"

"Gotta run a few errands. Take my car over to my mechanic, get it

[202]

tuned up, drop off a gift to my friend for her birthday. Why?"

"I thought maybe we could do somethin', go somewhere."

"After I get back, sure. What're ya thinkin'?"

"Okay... Well, have you ever been to St. Curvy's?"

He mulled it over. "You talkin' about that old English Gothic-style church on Woodward? Why would you want to go there? It's abandoned."

"Yeah! It's even *more* enchanting now! I dunno, I guess it's something about ruins that I find almost... spell-binding. So much history behind them, ambiguity. It's like they've seen their best days, retaining some of their former glory and triumph in their fallen condition, persisting on with us, never fully fading out. Like the train station downtown."

"Is that supposed to be metaphoric or somethin'? Christ, do you think I wanna think about death all the time?"

"Oh, well never mind then. And no, I wasn't trying to be metaphoric..."

"What about somethin' else?"

"Have you been to the African Bead Gallery, off 96 and Grand Boulevard? The glass walls, the sculptures made from iron, silver—"

"No, I don't think I have. You know, I really wish you would've went with me to the Meijer Gardens a couple of weeks ago."

After brunch, Bennett took his car to get it tuned up and then went to the bank to close his account, figuring he wouldn't need it anymore. Sara sat in his apartment, smoking weed, strumming her ukulele, watching the clouds shift through the sky. Her mind made out different shapes in the clouds: a turtle, Mickey Mouse, a rhinoceros, an Italian man with a bushy mustache, in that order. She looked through the boxes of books Bennett had left out on the floor.

"*The Suffering Savior*," she chuckled. "Hmm."

She also found a bag of old specialty coins and medals. They were items Bennett had minted at his shop in another age. She marveled at a side of him she'd never really known. After a few hours, he returned.

"Hey," he said upon entry, "ready to take me to that art gallery you were talking about?"

"Yep! Let's go! You ready?"

"Mm-hmm. Is this in a museum or a house or out in the open?"

"Outside.

"Good. It's a beautiful day."

She drove him down to the exhibit. They walked around, admiring the various structures local artists had created using simple objects and everyday tools: wooden fence posts, iron rods, coil rods, like the ones he used to make, broken glass, car tires, and otherwise useless junk.

"It's like they say, one man's trash is another man's treasure."

He agreed, absorbing a classroom display in front of him, a large cluster of twisted iron and metal surrounded by folding chairs with rocks sitting on them, the rocks painted with black silhouettes of heads, all of them wearing dread locks. The sign in front of the spectacle read: "'Iron Teaching Rocks How to Rust.'" He didn't know what it meant but he thought it sounded profound. Sara came and stood next to him and he put his arm around her, the two friends remaining there as the sun sank into the distance across the highway, cars speeding past, the air growing cooler. For a split second, time seemed to stand still.

On the way back to the suburbs they stopped at a pizzeria, both reveling in their final hours together, soaking up each other's company, the looming truth of reality tucked away in the back of their minds like old letters in a dusty shoebox. I love you, he thought, though he refrained from saying it.

By the time they finished eating, it was nearly eight o'clock. Soon everyone would be at The Showcase. Together they drove to the shabby hole in the wall. He surveyed the cars in the parking lot as they pulled up to the building, seeing Marty's and Dave's trucks, Fred's coupe, all of the other guys from Tuesday night poker.

"Hey," he said to Sara as they came to a stop. "I just remembered I was supposed to bring somethin' really important for my friend Marty. He's gonna kill me if I don't have it. I gotta run home real quick, it won't take long. Can you let everyone know so they don't wonder where I am?"

"Sure..."

She opened the door and got out. He moved to the driver's seat and gave her a long emphatic grin, a grin that spoke of regret and nostalgia, yearning and love. It was an image she would never forget.

"See ya in a bit, Ben."

She never called him Ben before and didn't know why she did

[205]

now. He waved to her and drove off. She walked into the drab atmosphere, noted a few people playing pool and shooting darts, and sat down at the bar. The bartender looked at her.

"What can I get'cha hon?" she asked.

"Um, I'll have a whiskey sour, please."

"I'm gonna have to see some ID."

She pulled out her ID, eavesdropping on a conversation between two men positioned a few stools down from her.

"Man, it's almost eight thirty and he still ain't here!" said a short, stocky man.

"I told ya he was gonna bail," replied a short, sleek man, sitting next to him.

"Um, excuse me," Sara butted in, "you guys talkin' about Bennett?"

"Yeah!" they exclaimed.

"He dropped me off, said he had to run home for somethin' important, uh, for his friend Marty I guess?"

"Someone say my name?" A tall and skinny man with short blonde hair and glasses approached. "Hi, I'm Marty," he said, extending his hand to Sara.

"Sara," she reciprocated.

"Oh!" the two short men replied.

"You're that neighbor of his," the one sitting nearer to her said, "the one he's been seein' lately. You moved in with him, right?"

"Shit! You're Sara?!" the other added, his eyes moving up and down to examine her feminine qualities. "Damn! Good goin', Benny, ya old mutt! I'm Dave."

"I'm Fred," said the closer one.

"Oh, it wasn't like that *at all!*"

"He isn't coming," the bartender said, setting Sara's whiskey sour on a napkin in front of her.

"What'cha mean, Jazz?" they asked.

"I saw Bennett earlier today. He stopped by my house to give me a painting, said he made it with you, Sara."

"Yeah."

"You guys know him. You didn't think he'd actually show up to this, did you?"

"What? But he was all excited to come out here, to see everyone," Marty said, sounding personally let down.

"C'mon," she continued, "the dude is dying, you think he wants all this? It's painful for him."

"Well, that's some bullshit," Dave snapped. "Fuck it. Sweetie, get us some shots, will ya?"

"On you?"

"Nah darlin', on the house. C'mon, somethin' strong, for Bennett."

"Alright, somethin' strong for Bennett..."

Jasmine poured them all shots of a fine, expensive whiskey she had on hand. Everyone raised a glass.

"To Bennett," she said.

"To Bennett," everyone repeated, raising their glasses together and at once downing the whiskey.

[207]

Sara sat there, disoriented, confused. He lied to me? she asked herself. How am I supposed to get home? She hung her head in gloom, trying to ignore the perceived idiocy surrounding her.

"*Look* at her!" she heard Dave whisper to Fred when Jasmine turned around get to more drinks, loud enough for Jasmine to hear.

"You boys are too young for me," she told them, setting their drinks down.

"Don't worry, he likes older women!" Fred laughed drunkenly, thinking he was being hilarious but coming off to Sara as totally pathetic.

"C'mon baby," Dave continued, "you and me, my place, fine bottle of champagne, lights dimmed..."

"Not the kind of fine champagne you're thinkin' about!" Fred interjected hysterically.

Jasmine shrugged them off and turned to Sara. "What's with the long face, kid?"

"Oh, ya know, my ride ditched me here, that's all..."

"Ah, I'm sorry, that—"

"I'll give ya a ride!" Dave interrupted, slurring his words.

"Yeah, and more than a ride *home*!" Fred added, now almost in tears.

Dave slapped him, giggling like a young boy on the playground. Sara smiled uncomfortably.

"I'll take you home," Marty chimed in, approaching the bar with an empty bottle. "Only had two beers, don't worry. Besides, it's kinda pointless to stick around when he ain't even gonna show. My wife didn't want me out too late anyway."

She looked at Marty and got a sense of his energy, then at Dave and Fred, their gaze like a pair of Neanderthal eyes on the hunt. Marty seemed safe enough.

"Sure," she said, "that'd be great."

The two drove back to Willow Lane in Marty's truck. Sara sat motionless, staring out into the night sky. Marty tried to lighten the mood.

"So, uh, you've known Bennett a long time?"

"No," she said quietly, "only a month."

"Hmm," Marty said, nodding his head. "We haven't talked a whole lot lately, not like we used to anyway, but the one time he mentioned you, he had only good things to say."

She looked at him. "Yeah?"

"Yeah, I mean, Bennett was the type of person who didn't really trust women, didn't trust people in general."

She knew exactly what that was like.

"But when he talked about you, I could tell it was good ol' Bennett, happy, being himself."

"Yeah," she said, "I can see that. You think he'll ever come back to Michigan once he leaves?"

"Oh, he's already gone."

"But he wasn't leavin' until tomorr—"

"Watch. He won't be home. He's gone. He's never comin' back."

[209]

Marty dropped her off, she thanked him and walked up the stairs to Bennett's apartment. Pulling out the spare key he'd given her, she thought about the day he lost his key, when they spent the afternoon eating lunch at Davis Park. It made her smile. She put the key in the lock and opened the door. Mya stood in the hallway meowing, the place completely dark. When she turned the kitchen light on, sure enough all of Bennett's clothes and boxes were gone, the furniture left intact exactly as it'd always been. She glanced over at the café table where a box sat, a notebook and a piece of paper sitting on top of it. She walked over, feeling renounced, removed the notebook and paper, and opened the box. Inside were wads of one hundred dollar bills. Seventy-five of them to be precise. She picked up the piece of paper, a letter addressed to her:

Dear Sara,

First off, I want to say I'm sorry for ditching you tonight. I didn't want to but I couldn't see going about it any other way. I hate these kinds of things, farewell parties, get-togethers in general, they always feel so contrived. I'm sure you know what I mean.

Sara grinned.

I had the most wonderful time with you today, this past week, the past month. If I believed in reincarnation, I'd say we knew each other in a previous life. Goodbyes aren't supposed to be hard for me, I've said far too many of them.

[210]

For some reason, I couldn't bring myself to face you. Besides, isn't this more poetic?

I can't tell you enough how much I appreciate you. You've changed my life more than this stupid illness ever could. You helped me heal. You allowed me to see who it is that I've always wanted to be to my daughter, my son, the kind of father I wanted to be as they grew older. Your love of life, your displeasure with people, your narcissism, your selflessness, in everything you are, you taught me something about myself. I'm like you in a lot of ways. We don't have to fear death any greater than we fear life and we don't have to fear either of them. I don't anymore. Every moment is a gift and I'll be damned if I spend my time worrying about losing it rather than cherishing what I have left! No longer will I squander any more energy worrying about matters that are ineluctably beyond my knowledge or outside of my control!

How can the godless face death? My answer: by embracing it for what it actually is—death. I don't have to delude myself into thinking that the dissolution of my cells is a gateway to my utmost pleasures. I couldn't even if I tried... And believe me, I've tried. How much more valuable does that render our brief time under the sun! Don't ever forget: this life is the one that counts. We depend on those who came before us precisely as our descendents will rely on us. What might humanity accomplish if everybody thought this way?

I left you my notebook of the dreams I've recorded. I never did get around to writing my story. Maybe you can store 'em away, put 'em on a shelf in your closet, read them every now and again and remember me. Remember that I was a human being with hopes, dreams, fears, a lifetime of experiences and memories.

[211]

Take good care of Mya. I know I don't have to tell you that. Give her lots of cat kisses for me. You're probably wondering about the shoebox full of cash. It's a lot of money that I don't need. I brought enough with me and my family is going to take care of me anyway. Don't lose sight of the goodness in people. It's there, even if it seems impossible to reach. Take that money and go somewhere, take some time out from work and school when you can... travel, enjoy yourself. (Make sure you find a good babysitter for Mya though, a car is no place for a cat!)

I'll call you sometime. Don't worry, I don't plan on kicking the bucket quite yet. When I get to Texas, I'll give you an address and we can write each other. Until then, your friend in life,

Bennett

Sara staggered to the recliner and sat down. She couldn't tell if she was in shock from trying to process the letter or tipsy from the whiskey sour at the bar. Mya jumped on her lap. As she held her, tears slowly began to fall down her face. Eventually, she was sobbing, clutching Mya, washing her fur. There was no question: Mya definitely had a bit of tiger in her.

The next morning she woke up in Bennett's bed, still a bit bewildered, unsure if she had dreamt everything the night before. Then again, she doubted it because she never slept in his bed. She walked into the living room. Beyond the furniture and basic appliances, the place was empty. The shoebox was on the table, as were the notebook and the letter. She fed Mya, got dressed, and plunked in the recliner. Sitting on the coffee table in front of her was the book Bennett had bought for her, *Cosmic Trigger*. She picked it up.

"I think I'm ready to get into this," she said to Mya, who scarfed down her chicken bits in gravy.

The sun illuminated the apartment. It was a fine autumn morning. She grabbed her jacket, the Wilson book, the notebook full of dreams, kissed Mya goodbye, and walked out the door. She went about half a mile until she came to Telly's, the hidden diner where she and Bennett had eaten breakfast together. Helping herself to a seat, she ordered a coffee and began reading about Bennett's dreams, doing her best to disregard the drivel coming from the elderly man seated across the aisle from her. He appeared to be babbling.

"Excuse me, ma'am," the old man said in a raspy voice when the waitress walked by. "I asked for some coffee and that other lady didn't bring any back. Jesus, what's wrong with you people?"

The waitress apologized and promised that she'd return promptly.

Sara turned to look at the man. He was short, tanned, had a bald, freckled head, appeared to be lacking teeth. She guessed he was probably in his mid-seventies, possibly mentally disturbed. He was watching the news intently on the one TV suspended in the corner of the diner. He glanced at Sara. She tried to look away but couldn't escape being noticed.

"Hey," he said pointing to the TV. "Did ya hear about that?"

She shook her head.

"Lady," he said to the waitress, "can you turn up the volume?"

Sara was becoming annoyed.

"Breaking news out of Virginia," said the anchorwoman. "As you can see from our helicopter cam, a *devastating* accident on I-95 about thirty minutes north of Richmond. Happened earlier this morning during the middle of rush hour. We're gonna go to Brett. Brett, what can you tell us?"

"Well, I'm being told that there were nineteen cars involved!" he shouted as the helicopter cam panned out to capture the breadth of the mayhem. "A horrendous wreck! Developments are ongoing but so far police believe a single male driver, driving a Ford Mercury, for some apparent reason swerved across his lane into a tractor trailer, which veered off and hit another tractor trailer, causing a domino effect, and that's how this whole thing started. Police aren't sure if that driver fell asleep or had a medical issue. It's still being investigated!"

"Did that driver in the Mercury survive?" the newswoman asked.

"I am told he did not! He died along with five others. I'm also being told that a mother and her two children are among the victims. Scores more injured! Simply awful!"

The old man turned to Sara, smiling, missing teeth and all. "Good for that son of a bitch!" he said. "They got what was comin' to 'em! People need to wake up!"